D1213281

The *Friendship Book*

of Francis Gay

A THOUGHT
FOR EACH DAY
IN 2009

D. C. THOMSON & CO., LTD.
London Glasgow Manchester Dundee

Most people walk in and out of your life,
but only friends leave footprints in your heart.

January

ON the threshold of this New Year my wish for the world is peace on earth, and may the earth turn its face to the sun, and its back on conflict and cruelty. For each and every one of us I wish tranquillity of mind and spirit, happiness and health.

THERE'S nothing more irritating than trying to do something new only to be told, "But we always used to do it this way!"

While there's a lot we can learn from the past, Nelson Jackson believed that you "can't do today's job with yesterday's methods and be in business tomorrow". And he was true to his words.

In 1903, at the age of thirty-one, Nelson accepted the challenge to drive across the United States, despite owning no car, having limited driving experience, and having no maps! The trip took two long, frustrating months, but he became the first man to drive coast to coast across his country in an amazing, modern contraption — the automobile.

Sometimes being successful means letting go of the past and embracing what the future has to offer.

Saturday — *January 3*

HAVE you decided to make any changes to your life this new year? If not, can I suggest one? Be kind.

I'm sure it sounds easier than a diet, or giving up a bad habit. Kindness always seems such a mild little trait. But it isn't.

Mother Teresa asked us to be "the living expression of God's kindness — kindness in your face, kindness in your smile, kindness in your warm greeting. Let no-one ever come to you without leaving better and happier."

Quite a challenge, you'll agree. But the world will be enriched because you have truly made an effort to reach out.

Sunday — *January 4*

TRADITIONAL NEW YEAR'S PRAYER

WASSAIL, wassail, to our town
The cup is white, the ale is brown;
The cup is made of the ashen tree,
And so is your ale of the good barley,
Little maid, little maid, turn the pin,
Open the door and let us in.
God be here, God be there,
I wish you all a happy New Year.

Monday — *January 5*

OUR friend John came across these words after drawing up a list of all the wonderful things he'd promised to do in the coming twelve months:

"A New Year resolution is something that goes in one year and out the other."

Let's resolve to prove that completely wrong!

FLIGHT OF
FANCY

Tuesday — **January 6**

TURNING over the page of a calendar, I found myself gazing at a superb photograph of a river in full flow. Why is it, I wonder, that so many of us are drawn to the sight and sound of moving water?

I can't explain it fully, yet I know from my own experience that a river can be both a source of inspiration and comfort, opening our consciousness to the great wonder of the world all around us. There are some beautiful lines from the poet Ritaihaku in this context:

The flowing waters carry the image of the peach blossom far, far away: There is an earth, there is a heaven, unknown to men.

Long may the rivers flow, and our hearts be healed by them.

Wednesday — **January 7**

WHERE'S there's a will, there's a way.
Where there's a hope, there's a chance.
Where there's a note, there's a song.
Where there's a beat, there's a dance.

Where there's a joke, there's a laugh.
Where there's a smile, there's a friend.
Where there's a bud, there's a Spring.
Where there's a road, there's a bend.

Where there's a hurt, there's a pain,
Where there's a loss, there's a sorrow,
Where there's a heart, there's a joy.
Where there is love, there's tomorrow.
                                    Iris Hesselden.

Thursday — *January 8*

OUR friend Chris often goes out walking with her friend, Mairead, and her spaniel. Yet while they nod and smile to the other dog owners they meet on the well-trodden path by the river, they just carry on their way without stopping.

The dogs, however, always pause to greet each other with friendly curiosity. Chris remarked on this one day, and her friend's answer made her think.

"The reason a dog has so many friends," Mairead explained, "is because his tail wags and not his tongue."

Friday — *January 9*

ON our old friend Mary's bookshelves are many "lives" of great men and women. She finds them fascinating, giving insight into the real people behind the public faces.

When someone tries to kill the most powerful man in the world it makes headline news all around the world. So it was when John Hinckley shot and wounded President Reagan. But what Mary missed in the news coverage and only discovered more recently were these words from his daughter, Patti Davis:

"The following day my father said he knew his physical healing was directly dependent on his ability to forgive John Hinckley."

How true it is that our deepest wounds, those that take the longest to heal, are often self inflicted, such as resentment, anger and hatred. Let us never underestimate the healing power of forgiveness.

Saturday — *January 10*

L OVE in seven words is found:
Think not of self but those around.
They will then be, not just others,
But friends to cherish, sisters, brothers.

Sunday — *January 11*

THESE days there's a host of things we can do on a Sunday instead of going to church. And if you've worked all week isn't that service just valuable free time put to no good use? No, says the preacher Ralph Sockman.

"Six days a week," he wrote, "I sit like a weaver behind my loom, busily fingering the threads of an intricate pattern. On the seventh day the church calls me around in front of the loom.

"It bids me compare the design of my days with the pattern shown me on Mount Sinai and the Mount of Olives. Some threads, thereupon, I have to cut, others I will pull more tightly, and most of all I renew my picture of the whole plan."

Monday — *January 12*

I READ these words one evening and felt inspired by them: *Laughter is the brush that sweeps away the cobwebs of the heart.*

We all need laughter in our lives. The problems of the world can be immense and we may feel helpless at times. The best thing we can do is to spread a little sunshine in our own small corner.

So today, do try to share a lighter moment with someone who seems to be in need of one. You and those around you will feel so much better!

DOUBLE TAKE

Tuesday — *January 13*

A FRIEND, who was going through a difficult time, sent me this story.

A man had four sons. He wanted them to learn to judge things carefully, so he sent each on a quest to look at a pear tree far away. The first son went in the Winter, the second in Spring, the third in Summer and the youngest in Autumn.

After they all returned home, he asked them to describe what they had seen. The first son said the tree was ugly and twisted. The second son said it was covered with green buds and full of promise. The third son reported it was filled with sweet, fragrant blossoms. The last son disagreed with all of them and said it was heavy with ripe fruit.

The father pointed out they were all correct for they had each seen just one season of the tree's life. He explained that we cannot judge people or circumstances until all the pieces are available to present a complete picture.

Remember, don't give up when it's Winter for you will miss the promise of Spring, the beauty of Summer and the fulfilment of Autumn.

Wednesday — *January 14*

WHEN the artist Yoko Ono was asked what her favourite and most uplifting work of art was she replied, "The sky. It changes all the time and has beauty and power."

How true this is, for behind the darkest cloud there is bright sunlight and following the dark sky of night there is always the promise of another dawn.

Thursday — *January 15*

HAVE you ever said in a slightly dissatisfied way of someone, "They are really lucky, not like me. Everything just seems to fall into their lap."

Perhaps at such times, we should remember this wise Persian proverb:

"Go and wake up your luck!"

Friday — *January 16*

THESE words were read at the funeral of an elderly shepherd:

Oh, give me the hills where the wind blows free
The old stone walls and the rowan tree,
Give me the hills and the call of the wild
And the old-fashioned cottage where I lived
*   as a child.*

The words went on in a similar vein, touching friends, who had lived more sheltered indoor lives, in a way they would never have imagined.

Could it be that it is at times like this we realise the fleeting value of material things? The unknown poet reminds us that, in the end, simple things such as health, freedom and a home where we are loved are priceless.

Saturday — *January 17*

IN Chinese, the word "crisis" consists of two characters — one represents danger and the other opportunity.

Surely there is a valuable lesson in this; no matter how intimidating or challenging a situation may be, hidden within it, if we look, is great possibility.

Sunday — **January 18**

WHAT makes a memorable preacher? John Wesley used to burn his old sermons because he believed he must always come up with a fresh and exciting message.

It has been said that a congregation should leave church saying, not "What a good sermon!" but, "I will do something."

One clergyman told me the best advice he had ever received was to preach, not because he had to say something, but because he had something to say.

Monday — **January 19**

WE all have times when things go wrong and life doesn't turn out the way we would like. Sometimes it seems the only thing to do is to have a bit of a grumble.

Well, we can settle for this — after all, it might make us feel better in the short term. But with the same effort and a different frame of mind we can turn an unhappy situation into something better — like the great musician, Duke Ellington, when he said:

"I merely took the energy it takes to pout . . . and sat down and wrote some blues!"

Tuesday — **January 20**

IF you would plant for days,
Plant flowers.
If you would plant for years, plant trees.
If you would plant for eternity,
Plant ideas.

Wednesday — **January 21**

WE speak with different accents
We come from different lands,
Our threads of kin and culture
  Are worked in different strands,
Yet still they make a pattern
  So intricate and fine,
That though we may not see it
  Their colours blend and shine.
And though we all are different
  Each life one goal should span —
To make our thread of being
  As perfect as we can.

Margaret Ingall.

Thursday — **January 22**

SNOWDROPS flowering in pale January sun gave our friend Helen great pleasure. The magnificent sight brought to mind this tribute to a much-loved flower:

At the head of Flora's dance;
Simple snowdrop, then in thee
All thy sister-train I see;
Every brilliant bud that blows,
From the bluebell to the rose;
All the beauties that appear,
On the bosom of the year,
All that wreathe the locks of Spring,
Summer's ardent breath perfume,
Or on the lap of Autumn bloom,
All to thee their tribute bring.

These words were written by the Scottish poet James Montgomery who was born in 1771.

Friday — *January 23*

ON Annabelle's sixtieth birthday the Lady of the House sent her a card that said: *Some people, no matter how old they get, never lose their loveliness — they merely move it from their faces to their hearts.*

Fine words to consider on a birthday and on other days too, wouldn't you agree?

Saturday — *January 24*

A NATIVE AMERICAN BLESSING

HAPPILY may I walk,
May it be beautiful before me,
May it be beautiful behind me,
May it be beautiful below me,
May it be beautiful all around me;
In beauty it is finished.

Sunday — *January 25*

"IT is better to wear out than to rust out!" You might think the man who wrote these words was a hearty fellow full of exuberance and energy, but no, ill-health had shadowed Henry Lyte most of his life. He was known as a man frail in body, but strong in spirit and he never shirked from good works.

Where did he find the energy to keep going, even while unwell?

There's a clue and reassurance for us all in the words of the great and well-loved hymn, "Abide With Me", which Lyte wrote days before his death:

When other helpers fail and comforts flee, help of the helpless, O, abide with me!

THE FRIENDSHIP BOOK

Monday — *January 26*

RUMMAGING through a postcard collection in a Dublin junk shop Columb found three pieces of Irish wit and wisdom, well worth passing on.

Worries are like babies. The more you nurse them the bigger they become.

For safekeeping put your troubles in the pocket with the hole in it.

Every good deed you do now is a golden thread in the blanket that will keep you warm hereafter.

Tuesday — *January 27*

NIGHTFALL

ON winter mornings not a sound,
Except the grey wind in the trees;
The hills left bare on empty ground,
The lakes and rivers left to freeze.

A squirrel ventures from the glade,
Looks all around in search of food;
Deer come into the fields afraid,
Then vanish back into the wood.

Bright stars appear, each one by one,
A silver moon climbs bright and full,
The day is over, almost done,
And it was treasure, a precious jewel.

Kenneth Steven.

Wednesday — *January 28*

THERE are no passengers on spaceship Earth — we are all crew.

Thursday — *January 29*

"O LORD, You know how busy I must be this day. If I forget You, do not forget me," prayed Sir Jacob Astley in the 17th century.

A simple prayer but one that can summon reinforcements of comfort and courage to all who may be facing great challenges in life.

Friday — *January 30*

IT had been a bitterly cold night, there was a thin coating of ice on the garden pond, and the distant hills were topped with snow. Bare tree branches were etched against a cold, clear sky; everything was silent. A misty, pale sun shone on bushes and the seedheads were dusted with frost.

Under the apple trees two blackbirds fed on the very last of the fallen fruit, while a robin, red-breasted and bright-eyed, perched on the sundial. The silver-grey branches of the magnolia tree were bare but their glossy, golden-green buds were already rich with the promise of flowers.

This was a garden in Winter with its unique beauty; a reminder, too, that it was merely resting, and that there was Spring splendour to come, a cheering thought on a January day.

Saturday — *January 31*

TRAVELLING by car towards the English Channel bound for France, young Oliver tried to practise his reading skills by calling out road signs.

He fell asleep just before entering France and when he awoke he caught site of the French motorway signs. Sounding perplexed, he said, "I think I forgot how to read when I was asleep."

IN SAFE HANDS

February

Sunday — **February 1**

WHEN I was reading my commonplace book, I came across this sentence: *Faith is the envelope in which all requests to God should be placed.* How true!

Monday — **February 2**

HERE is the story of some special sweet-tasting treats baked for Candlemas, the feast of the purification of the Virgin Mary, which takes place on 2nd February. These delicious boat-shaped biscuits, navettes, have long been associated with Marseilles and the Abbey of St Victor.

It is said that navettes are boat-shaped, because they were inspired by two events — first of all, the arrival in a small boat about two thousand years ago at Saintes-Maries-de-la-Mer in modern-day Provence of Lazarus accompanied by his sister Martha, and the two Marys of the Bible, and then the adoption in the 14th century by the craftsmen of Marseilles of an image of the Virgin Mary washed up on the shore.

She was carved from wood and rather shabby looking but wore a golden crown; she became known as the Protector of Seafarers, Our Lady of the New Fire.

Le Four des Navettes in Marseilles has been baking these biscuits since 1781 and they are still enjoyed today.

Tuesday — **February 3**

ROBERT LOUIS STEVENSON lived a short but heroically full life. Most of his forty-four years were spent battling against ill-health — something he referred to in a letter to Charles Baxter, a friend from university.

Three months before he died, Stevenson compared his life to living under Vesuvius and waiting for a long-overdue eruption, yet his parting line to his friend was: "Literally, no man has more wholly outlived life than I. And still it's good fun!"

In the face of such joy in life how can the rest of us do anything other than put our complaints behind us and live each day we're given to the full?

Wednesday — **February 4**

MOST of us were taught the "Three Rs" at primary school — reading, writing and arithmetic. The Dalai Lama's Three Rs, however, are:

Respect for yourself
Respect for others
Responsibility for all your actions.

That seems like a good Route through life to me!

Thursday — **February 5**

HERE are some wise words that have stood the test of time:

"Happiness is something that comes into our lives through doors we don't even remember leaving open."

Friday — *February 6*

*WHENEVER you're feeling in
need of life's healing,
To smooth all your problems away,
    You'll find that tomorrow can lessen a sorrow,
When friendship brings comfort today.
    It's hard to stop moping,
But try to keep hoping,
    For then you're most likely to find —
With new hope now leading,
    your woes are receding,
To leave you with real peace of mind . . .*
                                    Elizabeth Gozney.

Saturday — *February 7*

AT a school reunion Pauline attended, the headmaster took an unusual approach in his speech. He donned his gown and pretended that everyone was back in school assembly.

Then, after listing the recent and not-so-recent achievements of the school and its pupils, he invited everyone to sing. For once, though, it wasn't the school song, but first "Three Blind Mice" and then "Frère Jacques".

Next, he split former pupils into groups and encouraged them to sing both songs simultaneously. Finally, he explained that everyone had just demonstrated that even when singing different songs — in different languages — it is possible to be in perfect harmony with one another.

What a good way to achieve harmony in a school, as well as the world in general.

NATURE'S POWER

Sunday — **February 8**

DID you know that 8th February is St Cuthman's Day? He started life as a shepherd boy and it was said that he had only to draw a circle on the ground and his flock would not stray outside it.

As a youth he set out, pushing his invalid mother on a wheelcart. The cart broke down in Steyning, Sussex, and he built a hut for them both.

He then began to build a church and was helped in the work by a mysterious stranger. When Cuthman asked who he was he replied, "I am He in whose name you are building this church."

It still stands on the same site and the story of St Cuthman has never been forgotten.

Monday — **February 9**

"THE Eskimo has fifty-two names for snow because it is important to them; there ought to be as many for love."

Margaret Atwood.

Tuesday — **February 10**

SOMEONE once said, "If life gives you lemons, make lemonade." This is sound advice for every single one of us to keep in mind at some point in our lives.

Simply put, make the best of a situation, see how it can be turned around, and most importantly, learn from it.

Personally, I've "made lemonade" on many occasions and have always learned from the experience.

Wednesday — ***February 11***

WHEN Irene and Martin celebrated their Golden Wedding Anniversary they were pleased to receive a greeting card which had these words: *A successful marriage is not a gift . . . it is an achievement.*

That quotation from Ann Landers was not only a well-deserved compliment but, as Irene herself observed, true of almost any kind of successful relationship.

"We've had lots of happy times," she told me, "but there have also been a few occasions when we've definitely needed to make a little extra effort to be patient, and to remind ourselves of what we really like and admire most about the other person.

"But if fifty years have taught me anything, it has to be that I know it's worth the effort, whatever kind of relationship you want to keep strong."

That sounds like a golden piece of advice to me.

Thursday — ***February 12***

OUR friend John has met a few rich people, a few poor people and a lot of people who were somewhere in between, and he knows it is not the amount of money they have that dictates who are the ones who light up his life. His special friends are those who have discovered for themselves a secret summed up by the singer Joni Mitchell:

"Keep a good heart. That's the most important thing in life. It's not how much money you make or what you can acquire. The art of it is simply to keep a good heart."

A PROMISE OF SPRING

THE FRIENDSHIP BOOK

Friday — *February 13*

I LIKE the old story of a woman who goes into a shop and finds God behind the counter. She asks what He's selling and the Almighty replies, "Whatever you want you can get here."

Proving herself worthy of this opportunity the woman asks for peace, love and happiness. "But not just for myself. For the whole world."

She's expecting great things and can't help but be disappointed when God hands her a small packet. "I forgot to say. We don't sell the fruit, only the seeds," He explains.

In other words the whole world can have peace, love and happiness, but first we — you and I — have to sow the seeds.

Saturday — *February 14*

I THINK that I shall never see
A poem lovely as a tree.

These famous lines, the start of a simple twelve-line poem, were written by Alfred Joyce Kilmer, a young journalist. He wrote them in 1913 after a country walk and he dedicated them to his mother.

Sadly he died in action five years later in one of the last battles of the Great War. By that time his poem was widely popular and it is said that his comrades recited it for him as he lay dying.

A few years later the lines were set to music and the song "Trees" has become a favourite.

Sunday — *February 15*

"SUNDAY is the golden clasp that binds together the volume of the week."

Henry Wadsworth Longfellow.

Monday — **February 16**

WHY not make every day a "yes" day? Greet the morning with a sense of expectancy, for who knows what this new day will bring.

Make a choice to live in the sunshine and not the shadows, and to face head on anything that presents itself as a challenge. Why not decide to grow and stretch yourself, to listen to others, to learn new things? Expect good things to happen and be prepared to change.

Live every minute of this new day to the full. Each twenty-four hours is a fresh, unwritten page, a chance to start anew, so look up and say "yes" to the day.

Tuesday — **February 17**

SOMEWHERE

THERE is a place I'd be today
If only I could find the way,
It's in my dreams, I know it well
  Yet where it is, no map can tell.
It's just a lane, by dappled glade.
  I walk alone, yet not dismayed,
For close at hand a sunlit stream
  Runs clear and chuckling through my dream.
The air is warm and perfumed sweet
  By woodland plants around my feet,
And as I walk in silent bliss
  I know no other place like this.
And then I wake — my dream has gone,
  And yet its truth still lingers on.
One day I know I'll find that place
  And live e'ermore in perfect grace.
                    Margaret Ingall.

Wednesday — **February 18**

JOSEPH Wresinski, who worked on behalf of some of the world's poorest people, came to understand their needs from first-hand experience.

Speaking of one community he said, "They were as thirsty for dignity as they were for running water."

Yes, food and water are vital, but we must never forget the priceless gift of self-esteem.

Thursday — **February 19**

IT had been a particularly gloomy day when the Lady of the House came home carrying a large bunch of brightly-coloured daffodils she had bought from a local market.

"I know we'll have plenty of our own in the garden soon," she told me, "and I also know you admire the quality of patience but when I saw these, I just couldn't wait any longer!"

Admiring how their perfume and colour brightened the room, I have to say I was glad she hadn't. As Bern Wiliams once said, "The day the Lord created hope was probably the same day He created Spring." Certainly both seem encapsulated in a bunch of daffodils!

Friday — **February 20**

RESOLVE

EVERY day, no matter rain
Or cold or wind or my own pain
I try to do just one good thing —
For that's what makes a sad heart sing.

Kenneth Steven.

Saturday — **February 21**

OUR friend Jean says that our household pets have a lot to teach us — for example, they can help us to hold on to our sense of fun.

"Never miss an opportunity to play with your dog," she told her two grandchildren. "The pleasure of having a dog is that you may make a fool of yourself with him, and not only will he not scold you, but he will make a fool of himself too."

Sunday — **February 22**

MY friend Sam was reading about the origin of the saying, "Go the second mile." It's used now to describe someone who does more than he or she has to, but it goes back two thousand years to much harsher times.

It seems the Roman soldiers in Judea were in the habit of forcing local men to carry their heavy packs for them. However, the law forbade them from taking any man more than a mile out of his way. The followers of Christ couldn't beat the Roman army by military might but they had a greater force on their side.

Compelled to walk the first mile they would then "go the second mile" for love, showing the invaders their faith in action and perhaps converting a few along the way.

So if you find yourself with some difficult task in hand, when you'd rather be elsewhere, why not do it, and then go the second mile . . . for love?

"And whosoever shall compel thee to go a mile, go with him twain." (Matthew 5:41)

FAITHFUL COMPANIONS

Monday — *February 23*

"WHAT would you say are the qualities that turn an acquaintance into a friend?" our friend Norma once asked her family.

A true friend, they replied, after some thought, would be above all considerate, loving, generous and forgiving. Their words are echoed in an old saying:

A real friend is someone to whom you can empty all the contents of your heart, the chaff and the wheat, knowing that they will accept it all, keeping what is worth keeping and blowing the rest away with the breath of kindness.

Tuesday — *February 24*

APPARENTLY we are sleeping more than an hour less than we used to each night, in order to get up and on with another eventful day. At one time people retired at sunset and rose with the dawn but now, in spite of countless labour-saving devices, we live in a society where every minute, it seems, must be filled with activity.

In his poem, "Slow Me Down Lord", author Wilfred A. Peterson has a novel idea for taking the stress out of life:

Teach me the art of taking minute vacations, of slowing down to look at a flower, to chat with a friend . . . to read a few lines from a good book.

Perhaps we should start to take a tiny "holiday" every day. Make time to read a poem, admire our houseplants, or chat with a friend on the phone. And we won't even have to leave home to do it!

Wednesday — *February 25*

LAURA loves landscape painting but when she first took up the hobby she used to find her beginner's mistakes most frustrating.

"For a while I even considered giving up altogether," she confided to the Lady of the House. "It made me feel so disappointed, to spend hours trying to capture some glorious view, only to realise that I hadn't come anywhere near doing it justice.

"And then I came across a memorable quotation," she said. "It was from the pen of Samuel Beckett, the playwright, but it seemed meant for me:

'Ever tried? Ever failed? No matter. Try again. Fail again. Fail better.'"

Laura smiled. "Do you know, it really helped me to understand for the first time that no-one, however talented, can expect to walk the path to success without occasionally stubbing their toes on the way."

Let's try to remember these words next time we need a little encouragement.

Thursday — *February 26*

AT the end of Jim's street there is a business that specialises in all kinds of home renovations. Glen, the owner, has a keen sense of humour and often posts a sign outside with quotes and sayings.

One day passers-by could see these thought-provoking words: *Change the way you look at things and the things you look at will change.*

Good advice, don't you agree?

Friday — *February 27*

OUR friend Brenda's great-grandson was born prematurely. She visited him in hospital and found a very small baby, whom she described rather anxiously to the Lady of the House as being as "vulnerable as a little baby bird".

Her words made me think and I remembered a baby bird I'd found in my childhood. I put it into a box in the airing cupboard, and with hourly feeds and a lot of tender loving care, it began to perk up. Before too long, it was ready to take flight.

I phoned Brenda to tell her this heartening story, but before I could begin, she told me that the new arrival was responding well to treatment. Before long, young Jack was beginning to stretch his wings and he soon became a sound little fledgling.

Sometimes, with tender care, we can leave behind the weakest beginnings and look forward to a bright future.

Saturday — *February 28*

TAKE time to play, it is the secret of eternal youth.
Take time to love and be loved,
It is the Grace of God.
Take time to make friends, they are
the path to happiness.
Take time to laugh, it is the music of
the heart and soul.
Take time to give, life is too short to be selfish.

These thoughts come from a leaflet picked up by friends in Notre Dame du Finistère, a much-visited church in the heart of Brussels, and I'd like to share them with you today.

March

AFTER a Sunday service the clergyman stepped into the vestry for a chat with his parishioners, including our old friend Mary. She caught sight of a card tucked behind a coathook with a quote from Rev. Dick Sheppard:

A parson should light fires in a dark room and go on lighting them all his life.

"In my early days we literally took the coal along for many a poor body's fire," said our friend's clergyman. "These days with central heating it's not so common, so I'm glad to settle for kindling a warm glow in someone's heart."

Just as worthwhile a task, I'm sure, and something we all could do.

LOVE. How lucky are those of us who have it or have had it in our lives for even a little time. While your love might seem to be focused on one individual it is, by its very nature, a sharing emotion and just by being, it makes the world a better place.

Christina Rosetti, the 19th-century poet, described it well in the following lines:

Lead lives of love; that others who
Behold your love might kindle too
With love, and cast their lot with you.

Tuesday — **March 3**

ON the approach to Stirling Castle in Scotland there is a little stone-built house called the Boys' Club and on it are the words *Keep Smiling* and *Play The Game*. They're not part of a poster, and they're not painted on a notice board. They are in fact carved from the lintels above the windows, a permanent part of that ancient building.

Those rough stones with a few wise words are more than just architecture — they're rocks to build a lifetime's character on.

Wednesday — **March 4**

A FRIEND who plays the violin joined an amateur orchestra. When the players met with their conductor to choose pieces for their next concert programme he gave them this advice:

"Let's select some new pieces and some little-known compositions, but let's remember that audiences love the well known and familiar, as we do, and they should be a large part of our programme."

He added, "You see, it's just the same with our homes and our friends — familiarity breeds content."

Thursday — **March 5**

I NEVER knew him but I like the sound of the man who had these words on his gravestone in Yorkshire:

God, give me work till my life shall end, and life till my work is done.

Friday — *March 6*

JENNY'S husband has employment which involves frequent moves, so we were sorry rather than surprised to hear that she would be leaving our neighbourhood.

"It must be rather hard," commiserated the Lady of the House, "to have to keep leaving everything behind you."

"Well," Jenny replied. "I always make sure I take the addresses of the friends I've made but other than that, I try to look forward rather than back.

"I go along with the philosophy of Jan Gildwell, who said: 'You can clutch the past so tightly to your chest that it leaves your arms too full to embrace the present'."

And that's not bad advice for any of us, whatever our circumstances.

Saturday — *March 7*

AS our friend Bert opened his trusty old toolbox one day, he realised just how valuable its contents are.

Some things, such as a screwdriver, we use regularly, while other tools are needed less often for a variety of different repairs and adjustments.

Mind you, I would never have thought of a tool named Kindness until the Lady of the House reminded me of this tale. A wise man, it seems, once said:

"Kindness is a tool that everyone possesses but too many of us leave in the box. It should be taken out and used every day."

Something for us all to think about!

THE FRIENDSHIP BOOK

Sunday — **March 8**

SOME people "talk a good fight". Just such a person was a ruthless businessman Mark Twain met in Boston.

"Before I die," he announced, "I am going to make a pilgrimage to the Holy Land. I'm gonna climb Mount Sinai and when I get to the top I'm gonna read the Ten Commandments aloud at the top of my voice! Won't that be wonderful?"

"Tell you what would be even more wonderful," Twain replied. "Stay in Boston and keep them!"

Monday — **March 9**

LEAFING through an old almanac, I came across this advice from a farmer. He was looking out over his fields, having just sown what would, he hoped, become the following season's harvest. It occurred to me it might equally apply to any endeavour where we've given our best for a good cause.

"Now you just have to believe," he said. "That's all you have to do — just believe."

Tuesday — **March 10**

HAVE you been worrying a lot lately? Well, many of us do have a great deal on our mind at one time or another. In such circumstances it might be helpful to think about these centuries-old words:

"We are more often frightened than hurt; our troubles spring more often from fancy than reality."

Wise words written by Seneca, the Roman philosopher, who was born in Cordoba, Spain.

DISCOVERY

Wednesday — *March 11*

*T*HE dales lie peaceful, green and calm
   Inviting in the early day,
But there are hills for us to climb,
   They're calling us — so come away.
The villages are left behind
   And soon the trees begin to thin,
And as the footpath starts to climb
   We feel excitement deep within.

The shadows drift across the fells
   The clouds are moving overhead,
The sunlight touches hearts and minds
   And dances on the path we tread.
The valley lying down below
   Holds worldly problems, cares and ills,
But we have found our own escape —
   The quiet path towards the hills!

                                    Iris Hesselden.

Thursday — *March 12*

I ONCE read a diatribe against "the youth of today", saying they were lazy, disrespectful to their elders, wore outrageous clothes, styled their hair in ridiculous fashions and had no sense of public decency or morality. It was supposedly written on a tablet found buried in ancient Pompeii!

When modern life seems just a bit too challenging, try taking the advice of veteran broadcaster Paul Harvey.

"In times like these," he said, "it helps to remember that there have always been times like these."

Friday — *March 13*

IS something bothering you today? Has something happened to upset you and you can't get it out of your mind? If so, take comfort from these wise words by Charles Kingsley:

The world goes up and the world goes down,
The sunshine follows the rain;
And yesterday's sneer and yesterday's frown
Can never come over again.

Saturday — *March 14*

IT was a bitterly cold day, but when I bumped into Marie she was glowing.

"I've just come from the church," she told me. "Today is my day for arranging the flowers, but when I first woke up I didn't even feel like going outside the house. All the same, I made the effort and, just as I was finishing off the last of the arrangement, a group of visitors arrived. They were so admiring and appreciative that it really made me feel good."

As the saying goes, "A few thoughtful words can warm even the coldest day!"

Sunday — *March 15*

ONE Sunday, a visitor from Australia attended a busy city church which was famous for its preaching and good works. After the service when one of the congregation befriended him, he confided that he had come all the way from his homeland to find God.

"But, don't you see," came the reply. "God has gone all the way to Australia to find you!"

Monday — *March 16*

COLOURS

SUCH perfect gold, the daffodils,
 Which through the wild and windy days,
Still lift their trumpets high to praise
 The coming of the Spring.

Such perfect blue, the Summer sky
 That canopies the dreaming world,
While poppies bright, their leaves unfurled
 Turn faces to the sun.

Such perfect red, the Autumn leaves
 That spin from branches as they blow,
And set the woodlands all aglow
 Throughout the Autumn days.

Such perfect white, the snow that lies
 O'er all the sleeping Winter earth
Until at last, the sweet rebirth
 Of nature turns the year.

Margaret Ingall.

Tuesday — *March 17*

HERE'S an Irish wish, perfect to share with you on St Patrick's Day:

May there always be work for your hands to do;
 May your purse always hold a coin or two;
May the sun always shine on your windowpane;
 May a rainbow be certain to follow each rain;
May the hand of a friend always be near you;
 May God fill your heart with gladness to
 cheer you.

CHRIST

DAVID

HILD

CÆDMON

TO THE GLORY
OF GOD AND IN
MEMORY OF
CÆDMON
THE FATHER
OF ENGLISH
SACRED SONG
FELL ASLEEP
HARD BY 680

Wednesday — *March 18*

ON the days we all experience at one time or another, when one hundred and one things — or so it seems — have to be done immediately, if not sooner, try keeping these words in mind:

"The shortest way to do many things is to do only one thing at once."

They were written by Samuel Smiles, a doctor, writer and social reformer. He was born in Haddington, Scotland in 1812; his book, "Self-Help" published in 1859, was a best-seller.

Thursday — *March 19*

NOT long ago I came across this small gem of truth from long ago: "The only happiness is in inner peace." These words contain everlasting wisdom — such peace is more precious than gold or diamonds.

Friday — *March 20*

DO you ever wonder what makes a good friend? Is it the person who can't do enough for you, or the one who thinks you're just wonderful? Is it someone who shares your interests or someone who doesn't mind listening to your hopes and fears, whatever the time of day or night?

I'm sure all of these things can contribute to friendship, but for me a real friend is one who sees our faults, but chooses to stand beside us because they know we can be better than we sometimes are.

Henry Ford, the famous industrialist, summed it up this way when he said, "My best friend is the one who brings out the best in me."

Saturday — *March 21*

I LIKE words, they are endlessly fascinating. So, when the British Council conducted a poll asking more than forty thousand English speakers in forty-six countries what their favourite word was I was intrigued.

There were lots of good words to be found in the top twenty, such as cherish, blossom and tranquillity, but the number one word took me by surprise.

Then, when I thought about it, I was surprised that I had been surprised! What other word would possibly mean so much to so many people of different races, creeds or colours? It's the word that goes straight to the heart of us all.

It was *Mother.*

Sunday — *March 22*

HOW often as children were you perhaps told, "Don't do that! You wouldn't like it if they did that to you, would you?"

The Christian version of this is much more positive. "Do to others what you would like them to do to you." (Matthew 7:12)

This is far more demanding. It's not so hard to stop doing things. It's far more difficult — and far more rewarding — to actively do the things we would like done to us.

Monday — *March 23*

"BE glad of life because it gives you the chance to love and to work and to play and to look up at the stars."

Henry van Dyke.

FLORAL
FRAME

Tuesday — **March 24**

LAGUARDIA airport is one of America's busiest. It was named after Fiorella LaGuardia, the Mayor of New York during the Great Depression.

Acting as judge in one of the poorest parts of the city in the winter of 1935, he found himself forced to pass sentence on a grandmother who had stolen bread to feed her starving grandchildren.

He felt sorry for her but fined her ten dollars. Then he paid the fine himself and fined everyone in the courtroom fifty cents for living in a city where such a thing could happen! The grateful woman went home with nearly fifty dollars.

Mayor LaGuardia exemplified the difference between sympathy and compassion: "Sympathy sees and says 'I'm sorry', compassion sees and whispers, 'I'll help'."

Wednesday — **March 25**

WE'RE always being told to "look on the bright side", but it's one of those things that's often easier said than done.

If, however, you find yourself in a situation with no obvious bright side, think about Matthew Henry in the seventeenth century. Having been robbed on the highway he offered up this prayer:

"I thank Thee first because I was never robbed before; second, because although they took my purse they did not take my life; third, because although they took my all, it was not much; and fourth, because it was I who was robbed and not I who robbed."

Now, there's a man who could find a silver lining in any cloud!

Thursday — **March 26**

FACE each day with love and laughter
  Chase away all doubt and fear,
Always keep your chin up smiling
  Do not show a single tear.
Keep your thoughts both bright and cheerful
  And your worries send to flight,
Never entertain low spirits
  Keep the lamp of love alight.

                                    Kathleen Gillum.

Friday — **March 27**

OUR friend Ian is a keen collector of agates. These amazing stones are to be found in many corners of the world, yet all share a common form. On the outside they are gnarled and rather unattractive, yet inside they possess the most exquisite rings and crystals.

When I see an agate it teaches me a lesson about the way I should look at other people, not to judge the outside appearance too hastily, have patience until I've seen the heart.

Saturday — **March 28**

WHEN Kenneth lived in northern Scandinavia for a time, he used to go out at precisely ten o'clock on Winter evenings to watch the Northern Lights. He never knew what colour they would be — blue or red or green, but in the midst of twenty-four hours of total darkness, he looked forward to their coming as to the arrival of a friend.

It was something to carry with him through the long darkness of the day.

Sunday — *March 29*

I SMILED when I saw these thought-provoking words outside a church:
*The Bible is bread for daily use,
not cake for special occasions.*

Monday — *March 30*

ONE Winter's day Ella left a garden shed door ajar. Every time she went past she made a mental note to secure it properly so the elements wouldn't damage what was stored inside, but time passed and nothing was done.

Then the following Spring she went out to find something from one of the shelves. Just as she was about to open the door wide, she caught sight of one tiny, bright eye inside.

It was a robin, sitting on a nest; that wise bird had turned her carelessness to its advantage.

Tuesday — *March 31*

ON a boisterous, showery March day Gail walked round her garden, and caught sight of a few daffodils flowering in the lee of a wall, braving the cold, each in "a yellow petticoat and a green gown".

There is an old adage which says that if you find the first daffodil of the season in flower, you will have more gold than silver that year.

It may be just a saying, but seeing these golden-yellow "Lent lilies", the first daffodils of the season, made Gail realise with pleasure and anticipation that the gateway from Winter to Spring was ajar. It would soon be wide open.

April

Wednesday — **April 1**

ETTA Hillesum only lived to the age of twenty-nine before perishing, like many other Dutch Jews, in Auschwitz during the Second World War.

In her short life, Etta showed both wisdom and courage to inspire us all. The diaries she kept during the last two years of her life reveal neither despair nor anger, but a kind of acceptance, a loving desire to understand suffering and an abiding faith in the ultimate goodness of humanity. Even in the death camp she was able to write these words:

Sometimes when I stand in some corner of the camp, my feet planted on earth, my eyes raised towards heaven, tears run down my face, tears of deep emotion and gratitude.

These words live on to witness the fact that the human spirit can never be held captive to evil.

Thursday — **April 2**

HERE are several thoughts to share with you today:

Happiness keeps you sweet,
Trials keep you strong,
Sorrows keep you human,
Failures keep you humble,
Success keeps you glowing,
But only God keeps you going!

Friday — *April 3*

" **M**USIC washes away from the soul the dust of everyday life."

Berthold Auerbach.

Saturday — *April 4*

REACH out to the stars as they light the dark sky
Be they ever so far away.
Hold fast to your dreams and don't let them die,
Though they fade with the dawning of day.

Reach out to the stars, they are shining for you,
The moon is your friend in the night,
Majestically sailing the heavens above
And sharing her wonder and light.

Reach out to the stars and forget all the world,
The heartache, the hurt and despair,
And let quiet stillness refresh heart and soul,
The peace give you rest and repair.

Iris Hesselden.

Sunday — *April 5*

OUR friend Marjorie was telling us how she never needs anyone to tell her to "Have a good day!"

"You see, I just look up at a framed tapestry on our bedroom wall," she said. "My husband Jim spotted it while we were on holiday in Torquay one Summer, and we couldn't resist buying it. These words give us the best wake-up call we could ever have:

"Today is the day the Lord hath made; let us rejoice and be glad in it." *(Psalms 118:24.)*

Monday — *April 6*

A NEIGHBOUR whom I met one day was full of foreboding for the future. "I have just about given up all hope of a bright tomorrow," she said.

I told Maureen that there is always hope in the world, clouded over though it is at times. She can still see the expression of wonder on a child's face, enjoy the sight of a multi-coloured rainbow, find beauty in the colours of a flower, read a love story with a happy ending, or offer the hand of friendship to all those who touch her life.

Hope, I assured her, sometimes hides but rarely disappears. It gives us a reason to continue and courage to move on just when we are telling ourselves that we would rather give up.

Maureen, who had been so despondent only a few minutes earlier, left with the beginnings of a smile on her lips.

Tuesday — *April 7*

IT'S good to give the younger generation confidence in their abilities, but even better to let them know that they can put their talents to good use. Statesman Bernard Baruch had a very wise mother, whose words would influence him for the rest of his long, fulfilled life.

"No-one is better than you," she would tell her son, "but you are no better than anyone else until you do something to prove it."

Bernard took her at her word, and by the age of thirty he was a leading figure on Wall Street. Later he became a mentor to several presidents and carried on advising on international affairs, right up until his death at the age of ninety-four.

Wednesday — *April 8*

WINNIE lives alone. A tiny woman, her health is what you might call delicate, so after a particularly stormy night of blustery wind and rain the Lady of the House dropped in to see she was all right.

"Were you a bit scared last night?" she asked.

"Oh, no," Winnie replied. "I just lay quietly and thought of all those poor folk who have no roof over their heads or a warm bed to lie in. I put up a prayer for them all and, it's funny, but the storm didn't seem nearly so bad after that."

Winnie may be small but she has a big heart.

Thursday — *April 9*

WHEN Lorna turned fifty her friend Ruth gave her a birthday card that said: "Count your age by friends, not years. Count your life by smiles, not tears."

What a lovely way to welcome any age, don't you agree?

Friday — *April 10*

IF only the world had listened to the beliefs of the native Americans we might not today be faced with the consequences of the damage inflicted on our environment.

They looked on themselves as guardians of all trees, plants and wild flowers, seeing themselves as caretakers on behalf of the seventh generation yet to be born.

There is still time to learn from them and share their foresight.

BOATS OF MANY COLOURS

Saturday — *April 11*

THE egg, a symbol of fertility and life, has been associated with Easter for centuries. Perhaps the most famous Easter eggs of all were made by Peter Carl Fabergé, a French jeweller. In 1883 he was commissioned by the Russian Czar Alexander to make a special gift for the Empress Marie.

The first Fabergé egg had a shell of platinum, was enamelled white and opened to reveal a smaller gold egg; this then opened to display a golden chicken and a jewelled replica of the Imperial crown. Fifty-seven Fabergé eggs were made in total.

The tradition has survived and today children in particular celebrate by hunting for coloured and chocolate eggs to fill their Easter baskets.

Sunday — *April 12*

I'VE been reading about William Cowper. Born in 1731, this highly-regarded writer penned many of our best-loved hymns.

His words of praise and devotion did not come lightly, however, for despite his achievements he suffered times of severe depression which only his conversion to Christian evangelism made bearable. To me, this makes the words of "Sometimes A Light Surprises" particularly moving:

Sometimes a light surprises
A Christian while he sings:
It is the Lord who rises
With healing in His wings.

A touching reminder that even in the darkest moments, glimmers of joy and light can break through.

*Monday — **April 13***

I NOTICED the Lady of the House washing an old crystal vase which has been in our possession for a long time, and she handled it with extreme care.

This made me think about the way we look after the things we're fond of — a treasured book, an old photograph, a favourite piece of jewellery, perhaps. All wonderful things in their own way, but all are just sentimental objects.

Much more important are the relationships we have with others. They can be every bit as fragile and they need careful handling like that precious vase. One harsh word can break trust, bruise feelings or stifle affection, so be careful how you treat others.

*Tuesday — **April 14***

HERE are some wise words to keep in mind when we are worried: "How much pain have cost us the evils which have never happened."

They were written by Thomas Jefferson, the third President of the United States.

*Wednesday — **April 15***

ONE morning, as I wound an old clock, I thought about the nature of time. We can't see it, we can't touch it, yet it is there for us every moment of our lives. What we do with it, how we use it, is ours to choose.

One thing is certain — we can turn the clock back, turn it forward, even stop it, but time we can't alter. All we can do is to fill it in the best ways we can find.

Thursday — April 16

OUR old friend Mary shared this quote from Katharine Stewart's book "A Garden In The Hills" with the Lady of the House. In it, the author's love of living things shines through:

Days of stress, sadness or disappointment can be smoothed out as you look at the perfect structure of a flower.

How true! By observing the perfection of nature which surrounds us through the seasons, many challenging aspects of daily living can be put into perspective.

Friday — April 17

CHRISTINE had just arrived back from a week's self-catering holiday with friends.

"It was disappointing," she told me. "Our transport broke down, the cottage was cramped, and it rained almost every day. And yet," she added with a grin, "we had such fun. I know if I'd been by myself I'd have been miserable yet somehow, having friends to share the experience turned it into something that we could laugh about instead."

I hope Christine has better weather next time, and her experience confirms that there is nothing to beat good company!

Saturday — April 18

WHEN the sun rises, I go to work.
When the sun goes down, I take my rest.
I dig the well from which I drink,
I farm the soil which yields my food,
I share creation; kings can do no more.

Chinese Proverb.

Sunday — *April 19*

JAYNE had been teaching her young daughter the Lord's Prayer and Poppy would repeat after her mother the well-loved lines.

Eventually, she thought she could recite it on her own, so her mother listened with pride as Poppy carefully said each word right up to just before the end.

"Lead us not into temptation," Poppy prayed, "but deliver us some e-mail. Amen."

Jayne smiled, deciding to put her right next time!

Monday — *April 20*

TWO men went after one job. They were the same age, had similar qualifications, and on the face of it there was nothing to separate them. Which one should be given the post?

The boss outlined the drawbacks — the long hours, the early starts, the late finishes, the tight deadlines and stiff competition from other companies.

The first man's enthusiasm waned a little, but the second man beamed. "I love a challenge," he grinned.

"You can easily determine the calibre of a person," the boss said later, "by the amount of opposition it takes to deter him."

You can guess which man was offered the job.

Tuesday — *April 21*

DON'T make use of another's mouth unless it has been lent to you.

Belgian Proverb.

THE FRIENDSHIP BOOK

Wednesday — *April 22*

PETER was walking in a park near his house when he heard a familiar voice hailing him. Grant had been working abroad for years. Now, on a flying visit back home, he'd come to the park because he knew it was where his former neighbour would likely be on such a glorious evening.

They quickly caught up with news and then the friends shook hands before their ways parted again. Peter stood watching the sun sink to the horizon, filled with contentment.

As Herman Hesse, the German philosopher said, "When the paths of friendship meet, for a while the whole world appears to be our home."

Thursday — *April 23*

IF only life came packed,
With manuals we could read,
A list of clear instructions
And all parts guaranteed.
But oh, life's not so simple,
No useful hints or tools,
We have to muddle through it
Without the help of rules.
Yet one thing that we do have
Are others by our side,
To help support and cheer us,
In whom we may confide.
For as we share our knowledge,
So ignorance takes flight,
By working close together
We'll surely get it right!

Margaret Ingall.

Friday — *April 24*

WE all have our favourite quotations, and here is one of mine to share today:

Courage doesn't always roar, sometimes it is the little voice at the end of the day that says, "I'll try again tomorrow."

Mary Radmacher.

Saturday — *April 25*

RED Hat Society Day is 25th April. This social organisation for women over fifty years of age was founded in 1998; there are over one and a half million registered members in more than thirty countries.

The Society chose its name from the opening lines of the poem "Warning" by Jenny Joseph:

When I am an old woman I shall wear purple,
With a red hat that doesn't go and doesn't suit me.

The aim is to encourage fun, creativity and rapport and to develop a nurturing network for women in middle age and beyond. Their events vary depending on the group, or chapter as they call it; a favourite pastime is attending or giving a tea party.

Regional gatherings are called "funventions" and are held several times during the year along with official Red Hat Society events. Women often wear elaborate hats and outfits to these get-togethers along with a selection of feather boas.

So, if you are aged fifty or over, toss your hat into the air and celebrate! As the refrain of the society's theme song says: *All my life, I've done for you. Now it's my turn to do for me!*

Sunday — *April 26*

A PREACHER began his sermon by holding up a selection of fruit — an apple, an orange, then a pear.

"It's not Harvest Festival this morning, but I'm bringing you yet another fruit," he said. Then he held up a large card — written on it was the word *Sorrow*.

He continued, "I know that there are some here today who are grieving, and sorrow is something that we all have to endure at times. Try to remember this simple but, I think, helpful thought.

"Sorrow is a fruit and God does not allow it to grow on a branch too weak to bear it."

Monday — *April 27*

IT is often said that as one door closes, another opens, and it often does, I've found. An unexpected welcome invites you to pass through, to explore what is on the other side.

As the Persian poet Khalil Gibran wrote: "Life goes not backward nor tarries with yesterday".

Tuesday — *April 28*

IT is said that royal garments used to be woven through with precious gold thread which held the garment together. Pull it out and all the other threads would unravel, too.

Is this not like faith? It holds our lives together. Take that away and everything else loses its meaning.

We can't see it but the gold thread is there, guiding us on the right path, holding us safe from harm.

BEYOND THE HORIZON

Wednesday — *April 29*

IT'S often difficult to happen upon just the right present for someone, isn't it?

It can be hard enough finding a gift for a relation, a helpful neighbour, or the friend who seems to have everything he or she could possibly need. But when the Pacific Steel and Recycling Company in Montana decided they wanted to give something to their community, it must have seemed a formidable task.

However, they rose to the challenge and came up with the wonderful idea of funding their local museum of art to allow visitors free entry for a year.

This was a gesture that delighted both the community and those involved with the museum — they knew it would be the perfect chance to nurture understanding and appreciation of the arts.

Now that's what I call the perfect present.

Thursday — *April 30*

HOW thought-provoking traditional sayings can be — here are a few I would like to share with you today:

You cannot stop the birds of sadness from flying through your hair, but you need not let them nest there.

Choose your friends by the ear and not by the eye.

The gloomiest mountain never casts a shadow on both sides at once.

May

DID you know that the humpbacked whale "sings songs" which are constantly changing and evolving and will travel for miles underwater? It has a range covering eight octaves, with a series of high notes, and sounds pitched so low that humans can't hear them.

What's more, each song has a complex structure, almost like classical music, and may last for up to thirty minutes. It can be repeated for hours and amazingly, on any one day all the male whales in an area will be singing exactly the same song.

Not so long ago whales were feared or hunted for their oil and meat, but now there's a great appreciation of these amazing creatures and their incredible abilities. The whale is a perfect reminder to us that not everything is as it first seems.

HERE are some wise thoughts which you may like to keep in mind today — or any day.

When you arise in the morning, give thanks for the morning light, for your life and strength. Give thanks for your food and joy of living.

If you see no reason for giving thanks, the fault lies in yourself.   Tecumseh.

THE FRIENDSHIP BOOK

Sunday — *May 3*

WHEN I heard these thought-provoking words spoken by a young preacher I felt I had to pass them on:

"Jesus is the friend who walks in when everyone else walks out."

Monday — *May 4*

GRAHAM never fails to make me smile. He hailed me one day and told me that it was his birthday. Proudly he told me his age, too.

"I'm glad I'm over the hill," he said, beaming. "Now I can pick up speed!"

Tuesday — *May 5*

TRAVELLER'S TALE

ALL journeys are a pilgrimage
Exploring the unknown,
With travelling, adventuring,
Together or alone.
A voyage of discovery,
Perhaps a quiet time,
A chance for thoughts to wander free
And let our spirits climb.
Each journey is enlightening
With knowledge as our goal,
For we are travellers through time,
A pilgrimage of soul.
Our journey, when we first began,
Had wishes to fulfil,
So follow where your star may lead,
For we are pilgrims still.

Iris Hesselden.

HOME SWEET
HOME

THE FRIENDSHIP BOOK

Wednesday — **May 6**

THESE thoughts called "The Secret Of Success" appeared in a magazine over 75 years ago and they are still worth thinking about:

"Push," said the button;
"Never be led," said the pencil;
"Take pains," said the window;
"Always keep cool," said the ice.
"Be up to date," said the calendar.
"Never lose your head," said the barrel.
"Make light of everything," said the fire.
"Do a driving business," said the hammer.
"Aspire to greater things," said the nutmeg.
"Be sharp in all your dealings," said the knife.
"Do the work you are suited for," said the chimney.
"Find a good thing and stick to it," said the glue.

Thursday — **May 7**

THE Lady of the House and I decided to spend a morning sorting out our collection of photo and postcard albums — or at least that was our intention. Inevitably, the lure of "do you remember?" slowed us down so much that by lunchtime we found we'd made little headway.

"Never mind," the Lady of the House said. "At least I have the perfect inspiration for us — some words of encouragement from a writer called Margaret Fairless Barber:

"'To look backwards for a while is to refresh the eye, to restore it, and to render it the more fit for its prime function of looking forward'."

And do you know, I think she was quite right, for by the end of the afternoon not only had we enjoyed the job — we'd completed it!

THE FRIENDSHIP BOOK

*Friday — **May 8***

IF we are honest most of us probably think that we could improve in one area or another when it comes to daily living. We might want to be more patient, or more thoughtful perhaps.

We may try, but we are human and we shouldn't be too harsh on ourselves if we sometimes fail. Louisa May Alcott obviously believed it was the effort that was important when she wrote these words:

"Far away, there in the sunshine, are my highest aspirations. I may not reach them but I can look up and see their beauty, believe in them and try to follow where they lead."

*Saturday — **May 9***

EMMA's nephew and niece sometimes practise dictionary skills at school. They look up words, delight in discovering their meaning and use them to write sentences.

Martin Luther King Jnr. had a different perspective on dictionaries. "One day," he said. "Children from India will ask, 'What is Hunger?'

"Children from Alabama will ask, 'What is Racial Segregation?'

"Children from Hiroshima will ask, 'What is an Atomic Bomb?'

"Children at school will ask, 'What is War?'"

How good would it be, he wondered, if we could tell the children that these words used to mean something but no longer did? And that was why they were removed from the dictionaries.

One day . . .

Sunday — **May 10**

*O*N Sunday I sit with God.
  Side by side, shoulders touching,
 We make ourselves comfortable and visit.
 I tell Him about my week,
 My successes and failures,
 My hopes and fears.
 He holds my hand and listens,
 Sometimes saying little,
 But always listening.
 He tells me how dear I am to Him,
 How much He loves my company,
 That time cannot touch our moments together.
 Sunday is tranquillity,
 Tenderness,
 Solace.
 Sunday is green pastures and still waters
 Where my Father leads me.

Rachel Wallace-Oberle.

Monday — **May 11**

YOU might think that Sir Frederick Treves, surgeon at Bart's Hospital and physician to Queen Victoria and King Edward VII, would have held great intelligence in high esteem but in a 1903 edition of the "Boys' Own Paper" he gave this advice which surely applies whether you are young or not!

"Don't worry about genius and don't worry about not being clever. Trust rather to hard work, to perseverance and determination. The best motto for a long march is, 'Don't grumble. Plug on'!"

Tuesday — **May 12**

ONE of the most beautiful sights I've ever seen was when out walking with the Lady of the House and we were caught in a rainstorm. Dark clouds were directly above us, but the sun was shining and as it hit the heavy raindrops, they shone like jewels.

When I came across this Persian proverb I was reminded of that special day: "In the hour of adversity be not without hope, for crystal rain falls from black clouds."

What a refreshing image that conjures up, and I'm sure it will be a comfort to anyone going through difficult times!

Wednesday — **May 13**

I WAS intrigued to discover that the word "friend" has the same origin as the word "freedom". It just seems so right!

Where else can you be freer with your thoughts, your dreams and your feelings than in the company of a friend?

Thursday — **May 14**

THE artist Salvador Dali seemed to take pride in reckless living that shocked the world. However, late in life he painted his wonderful St John of the Cross, the magnificent work which hangs to this day in Kelvingrove Art Gallery in Glasgow.

It is one of the great images of the twentieth century, a painting that has touched the hearts of millions with its beauty and reverence. It was the last thing anyone expected of Salvador Dali.

Friday — *May 15*

MAX Ehrmann will be remembered for his beautiful "Desiderata", a wonderful piece of philosophy which begins: "Go placidly amid the noise and haste".

Sadly, his other work was almost unknown until the late 1960s, some years after his death. He loved nature, the moon and stars and the passing of the seasons. This is one of his shorter poems, but worth remembering when we are anxious about life's challenges:

Sleep quietly, now that the gates of the day
*   are closed.*
Leave tomorrow's problems for tomorrow.
The earth is peaceful.
Only the stars are abroad;
And they will not cause you any trouble.

I hope these words will give you sound sleep tonight — and in the nights to come.

Saturday — *May 16*

AS a young actor Laurence Olivier was given the role of a weak and foolish character. Olivier didn't warm to him and was making a poor job of the part. A famous director saw the play and Olivier's performance and spoke to Olivier who admitted he knew he was not at his best.

"Of course not!" the director said. "You don't love the person you are playing and you will never be any good until you do."

Soon Olivier loved the character with all his faults and was giving a great performance.

Love and understanding, they come hand in hand, don't they?

Sunday — **May 17**

" A WORLD without a Sabbath would be like a man without a smile, like a Summer without flowers, and like a homestead without a garden."

Henry Ward Beecher.

Monday — **May 18**

LOSING IT

I SOMETIMES lose my hankies,
I can't think where they go,
I sometimes lose my glasses —
I had them once, I know.
My gloves and scarves desert me
In ways beyond my ken,
And when I find the crossword,
I know I'll lose the pen.
I've often lost my bearings
When muddled by a crowd,
I've even lost my patience
Of which I'm far from proud.
But one thing I'll endeavour
To cling to till the end,
It's what I'd really hate to lose,
You've guessed it right — a friend!
Margaret Ingall.

Tuesday — **May 19**

R ACHEL, who lives in Ireland, includes these thought-provoking words at the end of all her e-mail correspondence:

"The only place where your dreams become impossible is in your own thinking."

Wednesday — *May 20*

I WOULD like to share with you these words of Antoine de Saint-Exupery, the French aviator and writer, who was killed in 1944 while making a reconnaissance flight over North Africa:

"Love does not consist in gazing at each other, but in looking together in the same direction."

Thursday — *May 21*

TOUCH — of all our five senses I think it is often underrated. And yet, of those five, it is probably the one most able to be appreciated by everyone. For most of us it is a totally instinctive reaction to pick up and comfort a baby or to soothe a small child with a hug, but it's an impulse we seem to forget too soon.

That's a pity for, as research in several universities around the world has shown, the sensation of a loving touch can make a definite and, they say, scientifically-measurable difference to our health and well-being. Experiments have shown that a familiar touch can even boost our immune system and relieve stress and pain.

So next time our instinct is to give someone close to us a hug, perhaps we should just do so — it may be exactly the medicine they need!

Friday — *May 22*

AMONG the many people who have worked towards peace in the Middle East was Tautig Zayyad, one-time Mayor of Nazareth, who once said, "I dream of a day when there will be bread in every mouth, a smile on every face, and a rose in every hand."

THE FRIENDSHIP BOOK

Saturday — **May 23**

"I DON'T need a friend who changes when I change and who nods when I nod; my shadow does that much better."

Plutarch.

Sunday — **May 24**

IT'S a story known across the world and brilliantly portrayed in the film "Chariots Of Fire". Eric Liddell was the hot favourite for a gold medal in the 100 metres at the 1924 Paris Olympics. Then he heard that the heats were to be held on a Sunday. After some tortuous soul searching he declined to run on the Sabbath.

His daughter, Patricia, has no doubt what would have happened if he had run. "He'd have lost. Something would have gone from his soul. He'd have broken something that was important to him."

Like Eric Liddell we can practise, train and work towards our goals, but without something to believe in we might never get away from the starting line. And because he adhered to his beliefs, Eric Liddell ended up running in a race he hadn't practised for — and set a new Olympic record.

Monday — **May 25**

DON'T just grumble at the dark;
switch on a lamp.
Don't just stumble over a stone;
lift it from the path.
Don't just tut over a wrong; right it.
Live positively!

Tuesday — **May 26**

CONSIDER these wise words penned by Eleanor Roosevelt:

To handle yourself, use your head; to handle others, use your heart.

Anger is only one letter short of danger.

Beautiful young people are accidents of nature, but beautiful old people are works of art.

Wednesday — **May 27**

OUR old friend Mary often visited a friend who had once borrowed a book from her. She could see it quite clearly sitting in the bookcase every time she dropped by.

"Why don't you ask for it back?" I asked, but she knew she never would. Mary's friend had simply forgotten that she'd borrowed it.

Sir Walter Scott must have had the same problem. Once, when he lent a book, he sent this message with it:

Please return this book; I find that though many friends are poor arithmeticians, they are all good book-keepers.

Thursday — **May 28**

OUR neighbour Stephanie has this Serbian saying framed and hanging on a wall at home. Its wisdom has made a great impression on all who visit, reminding us of our small, yet collectively-important place in the universe.

Be humble for you are made of earth.
Be noble for you are made of stars.

BIRD'S EYE-VIEW

Friday — **May 29**

I NOTICED these words on a poster outside our local church.

It's hard to stumble when you're on your knees.

What a fine reminder to spend some time in prayer!

Saturday — **May 30**

HERE are three memorable quotes from the wisdom of the Dalai Lama:

Live a good honourable life. When you get older and think back, you'll be able to enjoy it a second time.

The best relationship is one in which love for each other exceeds your need for each other.

Judge your success by what you had to give up in order to get it.

Sunday — **May 31**

IN several popular television series investigators use modern forensic methods to solve crimes. Inevitably, the solution to each mystery is in plain view, but only the experts know where to look for the answers and, more importantly, how to look.

If you are looking for answers to a bigger secret, the mystery of life itself, the answer won't be on television, but it's still in plain view.

The poet Robert Frost gives a clue about where to look in his words, "To see the world in a grain of sand and to see Heaven in a wild flower."

And the Bible gives us a clue on how to look in Jeremiah: "When you seek me with all of your heart, I will be found by you."

June

THERE is something we have to do but we don't know how to start, so we put it off . . .

When I feel this way I remember advice I was given years ago by a friend.

"There is only one way to begin a thing and that is to do it," he said.

It really is as easy as it sounds!

BE YOURSELF

TO just be yourself is the challenge of life
Whatever the world has to say,
Be honest and truthful in all that you do
And take the straight pathway each day.

The world may persuade you to
"go with the flow",
Conform or fall in with the crowd,
But don't be afraid, always lift up your head
And keep walking tall, walking proud.

The challenge of life is to be who you are,
There's no other person like you,
So keep your ambitions, your hopes and
your dreams,
Be steadfast, and watch them come true!

Iris Hesselden.

Wednesday — **June 3**

A CORRESPONDENT in London sent me these thoughts and I think that they're worth sharing with you today:

I am thankful for the mess to clean up after a party because it means I'm surrounded by friends; the clothes that fit a little too snugly because it means I have enough to eat; a lawn that needs mowing, windows that need cleaning, and gutters that need fixing because it means I have a home; the lady behind me in church who sings off key because it means I can hear; the laundry and ironing to do because it means I have clothes to wear; my alarm clock that goes off early in the morning because it means I'm alive.

Thursday — **June 4**

MORAG and Jimmy both came from shepherding families, in the old days when shepherds lived in cottages in the hills with their flocks. Recalling how they met and fell in love, Morag pointed out that during the lambing season they might not see each other for three months. The same might happen again in a harsh Winter.

Now in their eighties Morag squeezed Jimmy tight. "Absence makes the heart grow fonder," she smiled.

The Comte de Bussy had another way of saying the same thing which I'd like to dedicate to those couples who, like Morag and Jimmy, stayed together despite separation and hard times:

"Absence is to love what wind is to fire; it extinguishes the small, but it kindles the great!"

Friday — **June 5**

WENDY delivers the mail in and around a village. When I asked her how many miles she walks in a year, she calculated that it must be more than two thousand. Then she added cheerfully, "But when you look at the small picture, that's about ten miles a day — not unreasonable at all when you consider the keep-fit benefits."

To look at the big picture can be intimidating, but as Henry Ford said, "Nothing is particularly hard if you divide it into little jobs."

Saturday — **June 6**

ON a visit to a garden centre Anna read these words on a plaque: *Friends are the flowers that bloom in Life's garden.*

How true — even in the darkest days of our lives, the flowers of friendship will bloom brightly to cheer us on our way.

Sunday — **June 7**

HELP me to remember, Lord,
When I feel lost and small
That I am held within your arms,
And You won't let me fall.
Help me not forget, dear Lord
When hope seems far away
That I am always in Your care
And You won't let me stray.
Help me hold within my heart
The knowledge of Your care,
Each venture starts and ends with You
And always You are there.
                    Margaret Ingall.

Monday — **June 8**

LUCY was on her way back from babysitting, and looking rather tense. "My nephew's just started the temper tantrum stage," she explained. "I know he'll grow out of it but it does make life difficult."

Happily, we all grow beyond the "terrible toddler" stage, yet even as adults we're not immune to the occasional bout of rage.

And while anger can be constructive, providing the spur to help us change things for the better, it is more often due to placing our own feelings above those of anybody else.

I once heard it said that "a clenched fist cannot receive a gift". So next time we feel annoyed, let's remind ourselves to take a deep breath and open up our hearts and minds to the world beyond.

Tuesday — **June 9**

ENTERING a Tibetan missionary school Bob Pierce noticed a young girl, White Jade, sitting on the steps. She came every day hoping to be taught and fed but the school had no room for her.

Bob protested that they could surely make room for one more but the reply was they had already made room for one more, and one more, and one more . . . They simply had no resources left.

"What are you going to do about it?" he was asked. He only had a few coins to his name, but from that seemingly hopeless beginning World Vision came into being and millions of children across the world, including White Jade, have been sponsored, fed and educated.

That's the thing about "insurmountable" problems. They're often huge opportunities in disguise.

Wednesday — *June 10*

EVEN the hardiest of folk need a pat on the back every once in a while and a quiet "Well done!" might just make the difference between success and failure for many.

As Phyllis Theroux wrote: "One of the commodities in life that most folk can't get enough of is compliments. The ego is never so intact that one can't find a hole in which to plug a little praise.

"Compliments, by their very nature, are highly bio-degradable and tend to dissolve hours or days after we receive them — which is why we can always use another."

Thursday — *June 11*

THE future lies before you
  Full of possibilities,
Take that step and make the most
  Of opportunities.
New beginnings — set fresh goals
  And reinvent yourself,
Shake up all your good ideas
  And take them off the shelf.

Dare to dream and use your skills
  Think big — expect great things,
Give a free rein to your thoughts
  And let them soar on wings.
Take a chance and make that change
  Just show what you can do,
For only you can take the steps
  To make your dream come true.

Kathleen Gillum.

Friday — **June 12**

HERE is a memorable quotation from the pen of the French Impressionist painter Camille Pissarro. It is well worth keeping in mind:

Blessed are they who see beautiful things in humble places where other people see nothing.

Saturday — **June 13**

OUR old friend Mary always has lots of wonderful advice to pass on. One afternoon over tea as we were reminiscing, she said, "You can't control the length of your life, but you can have something to say about the width and depth."

Wise words and remembering them will help put each day into perspective.

Sunday — **June 14**

REBECCA'S son, Barrett, hopes to become a pilot. He has almost completed the fifty hours required for his private licence; then he'll go on to log over two hundred additional hours in order to obtain his commercial qualifications.

Sometimes he feels rather overwhelmed by the challenges of his career choice — not only is it extremely costly, it will take years to achieve. On these occasions she shares a verse with him that promises God has our best interests at heart and has set before us a destiny He intends to fulfill.

"For I know the plans I have for you, plans to prosper you and not to harm you, plans to give you hope and a future." (Jeremiah 29:11)

THE FRIENDSHIP BOOK

Monday — **June 15**

THERE'S happiness in simple things,
A butterfly with brilliant wings,
A calling bird — a rainbow hue,
The smile your baby gives to you.
The letter that the postman brings,
There's happiness in simple things.
The breeze across a field of corn,
The sun that lifts the edge of dawn.
A single rose, a trace of dew,
The blossom's drift, on grass astrew,
The crystal beam, the proud moon flings,
There's happiness in simple things.

Elizabeth Gozney.

Tuesday — **June 16**

"OH, dear," Fred sighed, "I do dislike these cloudy days." I was about to agree when I suddenly remembered an article I'd read about the formation of the Cloud Appreciation Society.

It was started in 2004 by Gavin Pretor-Pinney who even as a child had enjoyed the "meteorological meditation" to be gained by watching the different formations drift slowly across the skies. Nor is he alone, for within a few years the club was joined by thousands of people in many countries.

I'm glad that clouds now have their own special fan club, for they must be one of nature's most underrated treasures. Next time we see them in the sky let's try not to think, "Oh, no, rain," but instead let's look up and see just how breathtaking a cloud can be.

Wednesday — **June 17**

IF you're feeling down and the day seems pointless, I have the perfect remedy. Read these words — then try to see the world as this unknown author must have.

"This I know: I have planted a garden, so I know what faith is. I have seen tall trees swaying in the breeze, so I know what grace is. I have listened to birds singing, so I know what music is. I have watched children playing, so I know what happiness is.

"I have seen a Summer's morning, so I know what beauty is. I have seen a sunset, so I know what grandeur is. I have lived in a happy home, so I know what love is. And because I have experienced all this, I know what wealth is."

Thursday — **June 18**

I WAS reading about the challenges faced by the ruby-throated hummingbird. Most of these tiny birds winter between southern Mexico and northern Panama. The trip there takes them across the Gulf of Mexico, a non-stop flight of up to five hundred miles, which can last eighteen to twenty-two hours, depending on the weather.

The tiny, ruby-throated hummingbird averages about fifty-three wing beats per second in normal flight and has an average lifespan of three or four years.

When these brilliant, iridescent creatures return to a Canadian friend's bird feeder each Summer, he rejoices and marvels. Surely one of Nature's most amazing wonders.

Friday — **June 19**

GEORGE MacLeod was the founder of the Iona Community which has made the tiny island a place of pilgrimage for thousands.

A minister of the Church of Scotland he was famed for the powerful message of his preaching, as when he said we should "pray on our knees as if only God could change the world, and then get up off our knees and live as if only *we* could change it."

Saturday — **June 20**

"NO love, no friendship, can cross the path of our destiny without leaving some mark on it forever."   Francois Mauriac.

Sunday — **June 21**

BY anybody's standards, Alex's life has not been easy. He was orphaned young and raised by a succession of relatives which often involved him moving from one part of the country to another.

"Perhaps that's why," he explained, "one of my favourite hymns is 'In Heavenly Love Abiding'. It was written over a century ago by Anna Laetitia Waring but the words have always seemed significant to me, particularly in their total confidence that wherever we find ourselves, the Lord will be with us."

Wherever He may guide me,
No want shall turn me back;
My Shepherd is beside me,
And nothing can I lack.

And that's a promise to bring comfort to all who find themselves walking uncharted ways.

Monday — *June 22*

TESSA is always a popular member of whichever committee she happens to find herself serving on — perhaps because she has a sense of tact which would be envied by many a professional diplomat.

"It wasn't always the case," she explained. "As a child I was extremely outspoken, but then my mother wrote a rhyme to help me. I like to think that it worked!"

Just think before you start to speak
To criticise or moan,
For other people's feelings are
As tender as your own.
So always pay attention to
Another's point of view
And you will find, I'm pretty sure,
They'll do the same for you!

Tuesday — *June 23*

ALL too often we may hesitate to lend a hand in case we are taken advantage of. Temporarily, fear can replace generosity in our hearts. But what if you are, in fact, taken advantage of?

If you have kept your heart open, your soul generous and someone else has overstepped the mark, does it make them wise and you foolish? No, it makes you a giving person and them . . . not.

Referring to a legendary scam, Will Rogers, the cowboy actor and part-time philosopher was thinking along the same lines when he said, "I'd rather be the man who bought the Brooklyn Bridge than the man who sold it."

Wednesday — **June 24**

JULIE was lucky enough to read a letter written by one of the Prisoners of War who worked on the bridge over the River Kwai. Gunner Mitchell had just been liberated by American troops after three years of imprisonment.

The first thing he did was write to his sweetheart and when he reassured her he would be home soon the writing became a bit wobbly. No doubt it was an emotional thought. Then he wrote: "Home. What a wonderful word!"

We might wish our home was bigger, or smaller, or away from a city, perhaps. As children we probably took our home for granted. As teenagers often we can't wait to leave it. But when we're kept from it like Gunner Mitchell was — well, perhaps it's only then we realise that there is no place like it.

Thursday — **June 25**

HE who loves a garden loves the world
And the magic beauty there unfurled,
The excitement of the potting shed
*   With little seeds to put to bed,*
Pricking out those twin-leaved gems
*   Of fragile root and tender stems,*
Forget-me-nots and briar roses,
*   Primulas for children's posies —*
What calm contentment fills the air,
*   Tranquillity is everywhere,*
For he who fresh-tilled earth has trod,
*   Has laboured side by side with God.*
                            Brian H. Gent.

Friday — *June 26*

BURT LANCASTER played a trapeze artist in the 1956 film "Trapeze". The role probably came naturally to this actor who, before he came to Hollywood, was a circus performer.

However, he almost didn't get that first job. Asked to try out on the parallel bars, young Burt jumped to it — and fell on his face! Embarrassed, he jumped back up, spun, flipped, then fell off again.

The third fall, seconds later, took the wind from him, his costume was torn and he was bleeding, but he didn't have to try again. The circus boss shook his hand and offered him the job.

Not for all the times he fell, but for all the times he picked himself up again.

Saturday — *June 27*

IN novelist Neil Munro's "Vital Spark" series there is gentle Highland humour, while in "Erchie, My Droll Friend" there are many wry observations. But it was in one of Munro's lesser-known works that I came across some words well worth living life by.

In "The Shoes Of Fortune" one of the characters has been mortally wounded defending a child. On his deathbed he says, "Be good, be simple, be kind. 'Tis all I know . . . Fifty years to learn it and I might have found it in my mother's lap."

Sunday — *June 28*

*THOU art my single day, God lends to leaven
What were all earth else, with a feel of heaven.*
Robert Browning.

THE FRIENDSHIP BOOK

Monday — *June 29*

L AURA had seemed a little gloomy of late, so I was pleased to see her smiling. "I'd had a quarrel with a friend," she admitted. "I knew it was mainly my fault, but it took me a while to accept that our friendship was worth more than my pride. Now that we're on good terms again, I wonder why I waited so long."

Her words reminded me of something I read by Charles Williams:

"Many promising reconciliations have broken down because while both parties come prepared to forgive, neither party comes prepared to be forgiven."

As Laura would be first to admit, I'm sure it's much easier to accept the failings of others than to accept our own. But if we can manage to jump that hurdle, we might all become winners in the human race!

Tuesday — *June 30*

S OME readers can no doubt sing well enough to take part in a choir or even as solo performers at times. Others may feel that their singing is best done in the privacy of their shower.

Whichever group you belong to, just remember to sing, because singing, even to yourself, can fill your life with happiness. There is a poem which says:

*. . . When the night is come
And you are gone to bed,
All the songs you love to sing
   will echo in your head.*

Sweet dreams!

July

*Wednesday — **July 1***

OUR young friend Paul loves words! He's always interested in how words came to have their modern meanings and one day he found a new "word history" which I'd like to share with you.

The word *enthusiasm* comes from the Greek, as many of our words originally do. More specifically, it comes from "*en theso*", which means "God within". When Paul read this it made perfect sense to him, because with God within you the world and everything in it is a wonder.

And how can you not be enthusiastic about that!

*Thursday — **July 2***

SEASHELLS and seaweed
  In long, shiny strands,
Ice-cream and donkeys
  And fun on the sands.
Rockpools and starfish
  And bucket and spade,
These are the things of which
  Summers are made.
And though the world changes,
  Of one thing I'm sure —
Such pebble-bright pleasures
  Will always endure.
  Margaret Ingall.

Friday — **July 3**

AS human beings we have been given the dazzling gift of self-awareness. It is a wondrous thing to be able to stand outside our situation and think about who we are and what we are doing — this makes life such an exciting journey.

When we contemplate the Universe, it is even more wonderful to realise that the hand of God, the Creator of such immeasurable marvels is, at the same time, available to each one of us who needs help on life's journey.

Saturday — **July 4**

WHEN I have something to do that seems overwhelming, I'm often reminded of words Elizabeth Barrett Browning once wrote:

"Measure not the work until the day's out and the labour done."

It's a piece of wisdom that never fails to inspire!

Sunday — **July 5**

HERE is a prayer for this new week, by Robert Louis Stevenson, whose writing has long given pleasure to so many:

The day returns and brings us the petty round of irritating concerns and duties. Help us to play the man, help us to perform them with laughter and kind faces; let cheerfulness abound with industry.

Give us to go blithely on our business all this day, bring us to our resting beds weary and content and undishonoured, and grant us in the end the gift of sleep.

THE FRIENDSHIP BOOK

MOVING ON

*E*ACH day is a fresh beginning
For yesterday has gone,
Another chance to start anew
To change things and move on.
Another opportunity
To love and smile and give,
And act with generosity
To look up and laugh and live.

Each morning is a fresh, clean page
As yet unwritten on,
The threshold of an unlived day
But not yet walked upon.
So choose how you will live this day
As on your way you go,
For through our acts we all leave tracks
Like footprints in the snow.

Kathleen Gillum.

JUDY owns a shop called "Blessings". It's filled from top to bottom with an assortment of fine china, linens, scented candles, chocolates and many other hand-crafted gifts. The lighting is soft and soothing music plays — browsing through the shelves is a feast for the senses.

On the walls she has stencilled numerous quotes in flowing script. Here are two of my favourites:

Each day comes bearing its gifts. Untie the ribbons.
He who has imagination has wings.

Wednesday — *July 8*

*W*HAT hath God wrought! These were the first words ever sent by telegraph. But why?

As the inventor of the telegraph and Morse code you might think Samuel Morse would have every reason to feel proud of himself. He, however, saw it differently.

"When I was given acclaim for my invention," he said, "I knew I never deserved it. I had made a valuable contribution to mankind, not because I was so brilliant, but because God needed someone to convey this gift to the world, and He was good enough to choose me."

We might not make such momentous marks in history, but look around. Is there a soul who needs comforting, a wrong to be righted, a friend to be guided? Take the chance offered. Let Him use your talents. Then enjoy what God hath wrought.

Thursday — *July 9*

*A*NDY had just graduated as a teacher. It was a proud moment for, as he confessed, he had been a very slow starter in his academic career.

"I was the sort of child who believed that my classmates only achieved their high marks from good luck, rather than hard work. Then one year, my headteacher added a wise comment at the bottom of my school report:

"'Andrew is an able child, but should remember the old saying, *When you see a man at the top of a mountain, it isn't because he fell there.'* It was a very good way," Andy recalled, "of making the point that if I wanted to reach the top, then it would be me who had to do the climbing."

Friday — *July 10*

THE past is behind us, look forward once more,
The future is waiting, so open the door.
The past had its moments of laughter and fun
   But often the sadness obscured the bright sun.
Warm memories linger and love will remain
   But this is the time to let go hurt and pain.
Step out now with courage and new
      peace of mind,
Tomorrow is waiting, the past left behind.
                                    Iris Hesselden.

Saturday — *July 11*

MY friend Jill ends all her correspondence with these words: *Wishing you heaven in your heart, starlight in your soul and wonder in your life.*

May this be true for you today!

Sunday — *July 12*

DID you know that the second Sunday in July is known as Sea Sunday? First celebrated in 1975, Sea Sunday is now an annual event, an inter-denominational day of prayer and remembrance, not just for those who spend their working lives at sea, but also for their families.

I think it's an excellent idea to have a special day for mariners and those at home who support them. Sometimes it's all too easy to forget just how hazardous the oceans can be, and how much we owe those who risk their lives while working tirelessly far away from dry land. And I don't think it's rocking anyone's boat to say so!

THE FRIENDSHIP BOOK

OUR friend Don noticed an unusual inscription while visiting a cemetery. A small stone lay in front of a larger, more sombre-looking one. The large one had all the details of a life abundantly lived but the little one simply said:

Our Granny, who taught us to love beauty as much as we loved her.

Don thought about that for quite a while.

In the same graveyard there are much larger memorials to local men who fought in famous battles and businessmen who amassed fortunes in various trades. It started him wondering, would he rather be remembered as a brave warrior, or as a rich man, or as someone who opened children's eyes to the world around them?

It wasn't a difficult decision, and I'm sure "Granny" would have agreed with his choice.

GRACE was telling friends one day that an important occasion in her life was when, as a small child, she was taken to see the classic film "Snow White".

She said that what she had always remembered was the singing of the song "With A Smile And A Song", with the lyrics: *There's no use in grumbling when raindrops come tumbling. Remember you're the one who can fill the world with sunshine.*

"Somehow," she recalled, "I thought it meant me and so that's what I've tried to do ever since."

A simple but meaningful philosophy of life and one that's worth following, don't you think?

Wednesday — **July 15**

THE Lady of the House often quotes a relative who was well loved for her wise advice.

She recalled this gem: "There are three phrases it is best to avoid — 'What if?', 'If only', and 'Why me?'."

There is no reason why we should ever use any of these phrases again. Think about it today.

Thursday — **July 16**

DOROTHY was leafing through a photograph album, remembering faces from the past.

"You know," she observed, "Looking at these images makes me believe in the saying that there are people who come into our lives for 'a reason, a season, or a lifetime'. There are those who appear only briefly in our lives, yet mean so much.

"Others stay for longer, while the 'lifetime' friends teach us the lessons on which we build our whole foundations."

I hope that when we become "reason, season or lifetime" friends, each of us can play our role.

Friday — **July 17**

HOW many great achievements have begun as one person's dreams? Woodrow Wilson said:

"We grow great by dreams. All big men are dreamers. They see things in the soft haze of a Spring day or in the red fire of a long Winter's evening. Some of us let these great dreams die, but others nourish and protect them."

Look after your dreams, keep them safe. They are worthy of your protection.

HOLDING ON

Saturday — *July 18*

IT will be Daisy's birthday soon. "Are you going to have a party?" our old friend Mary asked.

"Of course," came the instant reply.

"You'll be inviting all your old friends?"

"And all my new ones," she beamed.

Daisy, I will have you know, will be ninety-five and is as young as ever!

Sunday — *July 19*

THE Lady of the House was reading Great-Aunt Louisa's scrapbooks and diaries. An entry for a long-ago July Sunday complemented by a drawing of a thatched cottage reads:

"I've just arrived back from my Devonshire holiday with friends. There were many beautiful places to paint there, and on our travels we visited Ottery St Mary, where the poet Samuel Taylor Coleridge was born in 1772. Since I came home I have been re-reading 'The Rime of the Ancient Mariner'."

Then follows these lines from the poem:

He prayeth well who loveth well
Both man and bird and beast,
He prayeth best who loveth best
All things both great and small;
For the dear God who loveth us,
He made and loveth all.

She continues: "I think these words come straight from Coleridge's heart, and I'm sure they will find an echo in many hearts, as they do in mine."

In the margin Louisa wrote: "The fruit of the Spirit is love."

THE FRIENDSHIP BOOK

Monday — *July 20*

THE Norwegians have a folktale in which Noah's Ark springs a leak midway through its days on the high seas. The dog is asked if he will put his nose between the boards to save the vessel and its precious cargo from sinking.

That's how the dog became man's best friend, they say, and it's also why his nose is supposed to have remained cold and wet ever since!

Tuesday — *July 21*

"GOOD morning!" our friend Alice greeted me. "I'm just off to work. Did you know I have a new job?"

Her words surprised me, for she had retired quite a while ago but Alice was quick to explain:

"I was finding the days so empty that I was beginning to feel rather down in the dumps. Then I decided to volunteer my services at the local hospital. Now I take round the tea trolley and chat to the patients, and love every minute of it."

Alice's words reminded me of something once said by that great American entertainer Ed Sullivan: "If you do a good job for others, you heal yourself at the same time, because a dose of joy is a spiritual cure. It transcends all barriers."

Now, you don't need a spoonful of sugar to help *that* medicine go down!

Wednesday — *July 22*

HE who can give has many a good neighbour.
French Proverb.

Thursday — **July 23**

CONSIDER for a moment the meaning of these Haitian proverbs:
A leaky house can fool the sun,
  but it can't fool the rain.
A stumble is not a fall.
  Wise words, aren't they?

Friday — **July 24**

I READ this story about a lecturer in stress management. At the end of a busy day, he picked up a glass of water and, instead of drinking it, he held it out at arm's length.

"How heavy is it?" he asked his students.

Guesses varied, and the lecturer smiled.

"You know, the weight doesn't really matter. It's what I do with the glass that counts. If I hold it for a few minutes like this, I'm fine, but if I were to hold it for hours, or even overnight, then I'd really be in bother.

"Life is like that," he explained. "We all have worries to cope with, and if we carry them with us all the time, we're going to be in real trouble. Sometimes we have to put our burdens down. We may have to go back to them later, but at least when we do we'll be refreshed."

So if something's on your mind and it's getting you down, just let it be for a while. Then if you do have to pick it up again, it won't feel so heavy.

Saturday — **July 25**

FRIENDSHIP is something that cannot be bought but can be treasured.

Sunday — *July 26*

I LIKE the story of the young lad who complained to his father that most of the hymns sung in his church were old-fashioned.

His father challenged him: "If you think you can write better hymns, why don't you?"

He accepted the challenge. The year was 1690, and the young man was Isaac Watts. Among his compositions are "Joy To The World" and "When I Survey The Wondrous Cross".

A story which proves the old adage that actions speak louder than words.

Monday — *July 27*

THE dramatist Jean Anouilh penned these thought-provoking words:

"Love is, above all else, the gift of oneself."

Tuesday — *July 28*

THERE are times in life when we are left feeling rather lost and things seem to get us down.

For many folk, a walk in the countryside gives a feeling of fresh strength to face life's challenges. This was perfectly expressed in these words set to music long ago by Jean Baptiste Lully:

Lonely woods with paths dim and silent,
A haunt of peace for weary hearted.
There's healing in your shade,
And in your stillness balm.
Here all seek repose
From the world's strife and clamour,
Find a haven calm and secure
And go forth strengthened and renewed.

THE FRIENDSHIP BOOK

*Wednesday — **July 29***

IF you have much, give of your wealth; if you have little, give of your heart.

Arabian Proverb.

*Thursday — **July 30***

ICE-CREAM, one of the most delicious desserts, can be traced back to the Roman emperor, Nero, who combined ice from the mountains with fruit toppings. King Tang of China created ice and milk concoctions. Recipes for milk ices and sherbets emerged over time and were served in Italian and French royal courts.

The dessert was imported to the United States and served to guests by such famous people as George Washington and Thomas Jefferson. In 1846 Nancy Johnson patented a hand-cranked freezer that established the basic method of making ice-cream which is still used today.

Then, in 1904, ice-cream cones were invented at the St Louis World Exposition. They appeared when a seller ran out of dishes and improvised by rolling up some waffles.

Today ice-cream is available in countless flavours and adored by young and old alike — one of the most delectable treats!

*Friday — **July 31***

GRANT me today the faith to know
That all I fear and all I need
Whatever place that I may go
Will always still be known to Thee.

Kenneth Steven.

August

Saturday — *August 1*

SOME days things work out well for us, but at other times we appear to hit an invisible wall that seems to block all progress. Well, here are two thoughts to mull over when you have a day of setbacks:

There is no failure except in failing to try again.
If you try, you might. If you don't, you won't!

Sunday — *August 2*

I'VE just been hearing about a music festival in which no concerts are held, no tickets are sold, and no seats ever reserved. Could this be the least successful festival in the world? Far from it!

I'm talking about the week-long annual Festival of Church Music which has been held at Priory Church in Edington, Wiltshire for more than fifty years. No concerts as such are given because all the music is performed within the context of the usual church services.

The singers, male and female, adults and children, are drawn from some of the finest choirs in the land, and are happy to give their talents freely in order to be part of this unique event.

It's Psalm 98 which urges us to "make a joyful noise unto the Lord" — and at Edington Festival of Music they certainly do!

POPPY DAY

Monday — *August 3*

WHAT'S the secret of a harmonious marriage? Ruth Bell, wife of the evangelist Billy Graham, was once asked if she and her husband agreed on everything.

"Goodness, no!" She seemed surprised at the very thought. "If we did there would be no need for one of us."

It's often these very disagreements — or rather the joining together of two people's differing opinions and experiences — that make a marriage stronger.

Tuesday — *August 4*

CHILDREN do it without thinking, but as we grow older we hesitate and often become embarrassed by the very thought. Yet there is no doubt that in times of trouble it fairly warms the heart.

What am I talking about? — simply holding someone's hand!

Emily Brough summed it up nicely when she wrote: "And remember, we all stumble, every one of us. That's why it's such a comfort to go hand in hand."

Wednesday — *August 5*

HERE is a message that has come down to us from a man called Gregory of Nyssa who lived in the second century:

The power of God is capable of finding hope where hope no longer exists, and a way where the way is impossible.

Thursday — *August 6*

ONE afternoon, the Lady of the House went to visit Elizabeth, a friend who is fond of writing verses in her spare time. It was glorious weather, so she wasn't surprised to find her sitting in the garden.

"I've a mountain of jobs waiting for me indoors," she admitted. "But how could I waste the sunshine? And at least I've written a poem while I enjoyed it!"

I know I shouldn't be here,
I've chores indoors to do,
But when I woke this morning
And saw the sky so blue,
It seemed the world was calling,
"Come out, come and play!"
With such an invitation
I couldn't stay away!
A perfect day is a gift to be cherished.

Friday — *August 7*

LEWIS TIMBERLAKE is a business consultant and inspirational speaker. He's been described as an Apostle of Optimism.

On his way to a speaking engagement he passed a small town with a notice at its boundary. It read: *We hear there's a Depression coming — we've decided not to participate!*

The weather might be miserable, the news might seem gloomy and people around us might be in a bad mood. We can go that way or, just like that little town, we can say, "No, thank you," and choose not to participate.

THE FRIENDSHIP BOOK

Saturday — *August 8*

WHATEVER your plans for today, there's nothing like a small present to cheer things up. So here's one for you — a few wise words all about giving:

Real generosity towards the future lies in giving all to the present. Albert Camus.

You must give some time to your fellow men. Even if it's a little thing, do something for others — something for which you get no pay but the privilege of doing it. Albert Schweitzer.

Sunday — *August 9*

TO encourage more people to come along and join his band of worshippers, a clergyman put up this notice: *Happy hour here every Sunday!*

Monday — *August 10*

OUR lives are full of precious links,
  Invisible, but real,
We may not see or touch them,
  Yet deep inside we feel
The ties of love and kindness
  That bind us to our friends,
To families and dear ones
  With love that never ends.
So cherish those connections
  And keep them strong and bright,
Their strength will hold and keep us
  Throughout the darkest night.

Margaret Ingall.

Tuesday – *August 11*

GRACE is often asked how she stays so bright and youthful. She always replies with a twinkle in her eye, "To stay young in spirit, keep taking in new thoughts and throwing off old habits."

What a wonderful way to improve ourselves a little more each day, whatever our age!

Wednesday – *August 12*

DAN was on his way to the travel agent. "Guess what," he said with a grin. "I'm going to book a cruise!"

His words made me think about all the explorers of years gone by – Sir Francis Drake, Marco Polo or Ferdinand Magellan, the Portuguese navigator who played such a crucial part in the first circumnavigation of the world.

It was in 1519 that he set sail westward through unknown waters, battling bad weather, lack of provisions, scurvy and a mutinous crew, yet succeeded in crossing the Atlantic then travelling down through the straits at the southern point of South America.

Magellan never did reach home, for he died in a fracas in the Phillipines, while only the remnants of his crew eventually returned to tell of their discoveries. Nevertheless, it's thanks to the courage of such adventurers that we know so much about the world today, can talk to and trade with other countries, and can travel to see its many wonders.

I hope Dan enjoys his voyage – and that he also spares a thought for those pioneers who charted the way.

Thursday — *August 13*

ARTHUR Conan Doyle, the creator of Sherlock Holmes, didn't only have a sharp mind, he also had a wicked sense of humour.

It's claimed he once sent an anonymous telegram to a dozen of the most influential men in the country, saying, "All is discovered! Flee at once!" Twenty-four hours later none of these men could be found.

It's a reminder that while some might have more to hide than others, we all have things in our past, or in the deeper recesses of our hearts which we'd rather keep hidden.

How reassuring to know that, from our distant past to the depths of our soul, all has already been discovered — and forgiven!

Friday — *August 14*

WHEN Greg retired early from a responsible job, he missed work far more than anticipated. The vague plans he had made to keep himself occupied seemed hardly worth carrying out and, as the weeks slipped by, apathy began to overtake him.

It was his daughter Jenny who came to the rescue. "She sent me a quotation she'd heard, which was exactly right for me," Greg recalled. "It said, 'What I do today is important because I'm exchanging a day of my life for it.' It certainly woke me up to reality."

It's a thought worth remembering, whatever our stage in life. Time is the most precious thing we are given on this earth, so let's spend it in the best way possible!

Saturday — *August 15*

" **D**IE when I may, I want it said of me by those who knew me best that I always plucked a thistle and planted a flower, where I thought a flower would grow."

These are the inspiring and memorable words of Abraham Lincoln who, in 1862 when he was the President of the United States, gave the slaves of his country that most precious of gifts, their freedom.

Sunday — *August 16*

*A*NOTHER week beginning, Lord,
    Another page to turn,
Another chance to start anew
    With lessons still to learn.
A time to lose all last week's fears
    And leave them all behind,
To look for bright horizons, Lord,
    And find new peace of mind.
Then going forward through the week
    Whatever lies in store,
Be with us on the path we tread
    And keep us safe once more.

                              Iris Hesselden.

Monday — *August 17*

HERE'S a thought for you to consider today. It comes from the many wise and practical words spoken and written by Ralph Waldo Emerson:

"You cannot do a kind thing too soon, for you never know how soon you will be too late."

Tuesday — *August 18*

BRAILLE is the famous system of embossed type that enables the blind and the partially sighted to read and write. The story of its invention by someone who was blind himself is fascinating.

One day, a three-year-old boy named Louis Braille picked up an awl belonging to his shoemaker father, but the tool slipped and he was blinded in one eye; later an infection caused the loss of sight in his other eye.

Louis was born near Paris in 1809. A clever child, he attended a school for the blind, where pupils were taught practical skills. They were also taught to read, but not to write. However, the method used to teach reading was difficult to master.

In 1821 Charles Barbier, a soldier who had invented for military purposes a system of night-writing using twelve embossed dots, visited the school. His system had never been widely used but Louis saw its potential. After a great deal of hard work Braille was born and in 1827 the first Braille book was published.

Braille has opened new doors of opportunity, enabling the visually impaired not only to read but to write, read music and even do mathematics.

Wednesday — *August 19*

ALONG the fenceline of my father's farm,
An ancient oak thrusts out its mighty arms,
A sentinel that disregards the wind,
And with unearthly height stands, sheltering
God's tender thoughts, the leafy, trembling young,
Who dream of reaching up to touch the sun.

Rachel Wallace-Oberle.

Thursday — *August 20*

"IF you are prepared to risk everything, you can do anything."

No, not the words of some great captain of industry, but Patricia Routledge, the well-loved actress who reached the top of her profession.

Friday — *August 21*

WE'RE all familiar with the term "guerrilla warfare" — but what about "guerrilla gardening"?

I must admit I hadn't heard of such a thing until I came across an article describing how small groups of amateur gardeners are getting together to reclaim little plots of neglected public land to turn them back into places of beauty.

This may be done quite casually, and often, for practical reasons, carried out late at night but, as one participant has pointed out, it's a situation in which everybody wins.

"The gardeners enjoy the work and the results of their labour, and whoever is 'officially' meant to be looking after these plots have their job done for them. Everyone gets a more attractive environment," she says.

It's a green-fingered phenomenon which is growing rapidly.

Saturday — *August 22*

CAROLINE Norton, the nineteenth-century poet and novelist, wrote these words, a description of true and lasting friendship:

"We have been friends together in sunshine and in shade."

Sunday — *August 23*

THIS amusing little piece appeared in a church magazine that the Lady of the House was reading:

There is a curve called confusion, detours called mistakes, speed bumps called friends, red lights called enemies and caution lights called family.

You will have flats called failures, but if you have a spare called determination, an engine called perseverance, insurance called faith and a driver called Jesus, you will make it to a place called success!

Monday — *August 24*

LYN'S aunt has a small plaque in her sitting-room and on it are these words:

My house is small,
No mansion for a millionaire,
But there is room for love
And there is room for friends —
That's all I care.

A reminder that whether our home is a cottage or a castle, it is meant to be shared.

Tuesday — *August 25*

ROSE used to have trouble living one day at a time. She is a writer and constantly looks ahead to deadlines and plans for future projects; she often felt she was missing out on today.

Then she read something Mother Teresa said and decided to try to slow down and look at life differently: "Be happy in the moment, that's enough. Each moment is all we need, no more."

Wednesday — *August 26*

*L*IFE is the flash of a firefly in the night. It is the breath of the buffalo in the Winter. It is the little shadow which runs across the grass and loses itself in the sunset.

Blackfoot saying.

Thursday — *August 27*

"I HATE sums," Ben announced on his return from school, "They're rubbish!"

It wasn't an auspicious start to the new term, yet all he meant, as his parents soon discovered, was that he was feeling nervous about facing a new teacher and lots of unfamiliar lessons. It was a cloud on Ben's horizon, yet with just a little bit of encouragement his fears soon disappeared as he began to take pleasure in his own achievements.

Of course, it's not just children who back away from something merely because it's unfamiliar. Next time we're beset by fear of the unknown, we should try to remember these wise words by William Penn:

"Help me not to despise or oppose what I do not understand."

And if we can do that, then I suspect we'll find things add up much better!

Friday — *August 28*

IF you find that other people always smile before you do, you are not smiling enough. Beat them to it: smile first. It won't cost you anything and you will nearly always get it back!

If laughter was made in Heaven,
The same two hands made smiles.

TOP MARKS

Saturday — *August 29*

MARJORIE, who is seven years old, likes to say a cheerful goodnight to everyone when she goes to bed.

"Night, night, Marjorie," the family echo from her grandmother, her parents and older sister, Jane. Then they add: "Sleep tight!"

Marjorie asked what these two words meant and this curious fact emerged. It seems that in William Shakespeare's time, mattresses were secured on bed frames by ropes. When you pulled on the ropes the mattress tightened, and the bed was made all the firmer to sleep on.

So next time someone bids you, "Goodnight, sleep tight!" you'll know the deeper meaning behind the familiar words.

Sunday — *August 30*

"THERE is no place where Sunday is more real than among the hills . . . if I went up silent, I came down singing — and that is Sunday in the hills."   Wendy Wood.

Monday — *August 31*

THEY say you can get too much of a good thing. Well, of some things that may be true, but can you have too much happiness, too deep a sense of contentment? I will take as much of these as it pleases God to give me and thank Him for it.

And what about beauty? Can we ever have too much of that? Can we give or receive too much friendship?

When it comes to the really important things in life, our souls always have room for more.

September

Tuesday — *September 1*

OUR friend Tim is no longer young but he made a two hundred and fifty mile round trip to hang up some nesting boxes in a tree in his daughter's garden.

"That's quite a journey just to put up bird boxes!" I commented.

"Well, it's more than that, Francis," he said. "You see, I promised my young grandson that I would have them in place before the nesting season and I didn't want him to be disappointed or to think I'd forgotten about it.

"After all, if you break a promise to a child, you will lose face but more importantly, *they* will lose faith."

Wise words indeed.

Wednesday — *September 2*

I'D like to share some words from the writings of a distinguished churchman, Cardinal Mercier, with you today:

In order to unite with one another,
we must love one another.
In order to love one another,
we must know one another.
In order to know one another,
we must meet one another.

Thursday — *September 3*

WHEN the Lady of the House met Carol for coffee recently, she asked how her elderly mother was.

"She's very well," replied Carol. "I took her to the 'Antiques Roadshow' when it came to town the other day." She laughed, then added, "Well, maybe I shouldn't put it that way, because she wouldn't like me making her sound like the antique!"

After a pause, Carol added thoughtfully, "Come to think of it, that's not such a strange comparison. Mother is my most treasured possession, and a rare work of art. I don't need an expert to tell me that, and I wouldn't part with her for all the money in the world."

Carol's mother may not like being called an antique, however lightheartedly, but one thing is certain — she must be delighted to know how precious she is to her daughter.

Friday — *September 4*

YOU'RE feeling rather frazzled,
  But the world won't go away?
You're worried by a workload
  That grows and grows each day?
Then make a little "Me-Time",
  Take moments in your life,
To find a calm oasis
  From problems, gloom and strife.
For though it may seem funny,
  You'll find it's very true —
You'll have more time for others
  If you make time for you.

                                    Margaret Ingall.

BLUE SKYE

Saturday — **September 5**

A FRIEND of mine who once hit a bad patch in life puts his current run of success down to having adopted this straightforward thought:

"I can't do it" never yet accomplished anything but "I will try" has worked wonders.

Simple perhaps, but surprisingly effective.

Sunday — **September 6**

WHEN crocodile hunter Steve Irwin died in September 2006, millions of people were deeply saddened. The forty-four-year-old Australian conservationist and television personality was killed when the barb of a stingray pierced his chest while filming on the Great Barrier Reef.

A story has circulated, however, that sheds a surprisingly bright light on this tragedy. According to reports from Australia, Steve's wife Teri and their two children had been attending a small church in Beerwah, where they lived.

Just a month or so before Steve died, he started accompanying his family to church and accepted Christ into his life during an altar call. He was later quoted as saying those were the best weeks of his life.

Something for us all to think about today.

Monday — **September 7**

I LIKE this saying which a reader in Norway sent to me: *There's no point crossing the river to get water.* It's true that we often overlook the blessings that are right in front of us.

Just take a close look!

Tuesday — *September 8*

MUCH has been said and written over the years on the theme of separation, but I particularly like this thought from the author Richard Bach:

"Can miles truly separate you from friends . . . If you want to be with someone you love, aren't you already there?"

Wednesday — *September 9*

*F*ORGED *in the fire* — that was the phrase used by our old friend Mary's mother to describe someone she felt had faced adversity and come out a stronger person. She would certainly have felt it applied to John McCarthy, the English journalist kidnapped in war-torn Beirut in 1986.

Five long years of imprisonment were to follow, a time which included long periods of isolation, extreme physical discomfort and the constant knowledge that at any moment his captors might decide to kill him. It was in the first months of solitary internment that John McCarthy reached his lowest point.

Then one night, lost in despair, he felt himself overwhelmed by a loving spiritual presence, filling him with courage and confidence in his ability to survive. Soon afterwards he found himself moved again, this time to share a cell with another hostage, Irishman Brian Keenan. Together they found the strength to get through each day — a strength that they were to need for another four long years before their sudden release.

"In the most inhuman of circumstances men grow and deepen in humanity," Keenan said afterwards. Forged in the fire indeed!

THE FRIENDSHIP BOOK

Thursday — *September 10*

FOR most of us sculpting a work of art would seem like an impossible task. But Auguste Rodin, creator of "The Thinker" and "The Burghers of Calais", had some surprisingly simple advice for an admirer who insisted the work must be incredibly difficult.

"Not at all," he replied. "You simply buy a block of marble and chip away at what you don't want."

We are, each of us, works of art, but all too often we hide our true natures behind habits of fear, self-interest or laziness.

I think Rodin might have had a point. Now, where did I leave my hammer and chisel?

Friday — *September 11*

A MILLION stars are beginning to fade,
The slim, crescent moon sails away,
The blackbird wakes early, his notes crystal clear
He sings at the gate of the day.

And stirring from slumber our dreams disappear
And soon the new dawn will begin,
The peace holds us gently, with silence around,
Restoring the spirit within.

The sky growing lighter, the morning awakes
And life can no longer delay,
And so going forward, new hope in our heart,
We step through the gate of the day.

Iris Hesselden.

Saturday — *September 12*

LAUGHTER is a smile with the volume turned up.

Sunday — *September 13*

EVERY Autumn a unique event is held in Elmira, Ontario. Pet owners bring their dogs, cats, hamsters, rabbits and other creatures into local churches for a special ceremony called The Blessing of Pets. Over each animal, this prayer is uttered in remembrance of St. Francis of Assisi's love for all creatures:

Blessed are you, Lord God, maker of all living creatures. You called forth fish in the sea, birds in the air and animals on the land. You inspired St Francis to call all of them his brothers and sisters.

We ask you to bless this pet. By the power of your love, enable it to live according to your plan. May we always praise you for all your beauty in creation. Blessed are you, Lord our God, in all your creatures! Amen.

Those who own pets believe the love between humans and animals is a spiritual experience that mirrors our relationship with the Creator. As George Eliot said, "Animals are such agreeable friends; they ask no questions, they pass no criticisms."

Monday — *September 14*

THE pages of my commonplace book are a colourful patchwork of all sorts of quotes and sayings gathered together over many years. They contain words to comfort, to uplift and to encourage.

I have written on the first page these words by the poet John Keats:

They shall be accounted poet kings, who simply tell the most heart-warming things.

Tuesday — *September 15*

WHILE out shopping one day the Lady of the House caught sight of this verse framed and ready to hang. She bought it and every time I catch sight of it I'm reminded how precious and intricate life and relationships are.

We are all of us from birth to death
Guests at a table which we did not spread.
The sun, the earth, love, friends,
Our very breath are parts of this banquet . . .

Rebecca Harding Davis (1831-1910)

Wednesday — *September 16*

DO you remember the drab station refreshment room in the film "Brief Encounter"? The poignant scenes between Trevor Howard and Celia Johnston are amongst the most famous in British cinema.

The station used was Carnforth in Lancashire, and as time passed after the film was made the room began to fall into decay. However, it was saved by a group of enterprising people who had it restored exactly as it looked in the film — even the original cash register was brought back.

Today you can visit the Brief Encounter Refreshment Room, which is now part of a visitor centre and sit at one of the tables just like "Laura" and "Alec" did in the much-loved 1945 classic production.

Thursday — *September 17*

A LOVING heart is the beginning of all knowledge. Thomas Carlyle.

THE FRIENDSHIP BOOK

Friday — *September 18*

HAVE you heard the story about a wise woman who found a precious stone in a mountain stream? The next day she met a traveller who was hungry and she opened her bag to share her food.

The traveller saw the precious stone and asked the woman to give it to him. She did and he left, rejoicing in his good fortune. He knew the stone was worth enough to make him very wealthy. But a few days later he returned.

"I've been thinking," the traveller said humbly. "I know how valuable the stone is, but I give it back in the hope that you can give me something even more precious. Give me what you have within you that enabled you to give me the stone."

Saturday — *September 19*

MAKE your day a masterpiece
And do your very best,
Put your whole self into it
With energy and zest.
Look up and laugh, be positive
Say "yes" to this new day,
Turn problems into challenges
To spur you on your way.

Welcome opportunities
That knock upon your door,
As stepping stones to better things
And learning something more.
Be bold, be strong, have confidence
To hold on and come through,
So make this day a masterpiece
And to yourself be true.

Kathleen Gillum.

Sunday — *September 20*

IN a world where famine is all too common our Harvest Festivals with their magnificent displays of sheaves of corn, specially-baked bread and fruit are reminders of our good fortune.

Harvest Festivals as we know them are said to date from 1843, when the Rev. Robert Hawker, Rector of Morwenston Church in Cornwall, invited his parishioners to a new service in September:

"Let us gather together in the chancel of our church, and there receive, in the bread of the new corn, that blessed sacrament which was ordained to strengthen and refresh our souls."

Robert Hawker was devoted to his seaside parish — there had been no vicar at Morwenston for over a century until he arrived.

Not least, he was also a writer and poet, and his "Song Of The Western Men" became Cornwall's National Anthem.

Monday — *September 21*

SANDRA received these wishes from a friend and I'd like to share them with you:
Today I wish you a day of ordinary miracles;
A fresh pot of tea you didn't have to make yourself,
An unexpected phone call from an old friend,
Green traffic lights on your way to work.
Today I wish you a day of little things to rejoice in;
The fastest queue at the supermarket,
A good singalong song on the radio,
Your keys right where you look.
Today I wish you happiness and little bite-size
*   pieces of perfection*
A day of simple pleasures, happiness and joy!

STRAWBERRY ICE

Tuesday — *September 22*

"I KNOW I didn't do very well in my school tests," Anna said with a rueful sigh. "But at least I did better than Joanne."

It's an instinctive reaction, to judge ourselves only by comparison with others, so few of us would view Anna's attitude too harshly. All the same, I prefer the attitude expressed by William Faulkner, winner of the 1949 Nobel Prize for Literature, who wrote:

"Always dream and shoot higher than you can do. Don't bother just to be better than your contemporaries or predecessors. Try to be better than yourself."

That sounds like advice from a man who knew exactly what he was talking about.

Wednesday — *September 23*

HERE'S a thought-provoking message that came into our friend Linda's e-mail box:

A comma is used to set off some element of a sentence from what preceded it, or followed it, or both. A comma is also used to separate two elements in the same way a person might pause when speaking. A period simply means the end.

In life, a mistake places itself between what precedes it and what follows. It's a pause, a chance to bring our lives back into alignment. Just as a comma is a tool for making the written words easier to understand, a mistake is a learning tool we can use to change the direction life has taken.

And an unknown author once said, "Let your mistakes be a comma and not a period."

Thursday — *September 24*

JEFF was just leaving his house when I caught sight of him, and I could see he was dressed for a day's walking.

"There's nothing like a good ramble to clear the mind and raise the spirits," he smiled. "Even if I don't always know exactly where I'm going when I set off!"

His comments reminded me of the thoughts of the writer and ecologist Edward Abbey, who said, "That's the best thing about walking, the journey itself. It doesn't matter whether you get where you're going or not . . . Every good hike brings you eventually back home. Right where you started."

I like that concept, for I'm sure it's true of any journey, whether it's of mind, body or soul. We all arrive back home eventually.

Friday — *September 25*

I ONCE read that "The garment of friendship is knitted on the needles of give and take."

What is so enduring about true friendship is that our friends know and see our faults and weaknesses and still like us in spite of them. Friendship, however, is a two-way concept. To have a friend you must be a friend — giving is as important as receiving.

In the words of an old Indian proverb: "For the friendship of two, the patience of one is necessary." And love and trust are every bit as important as patience in the knitting pattern of friendship.

It adds immeasurably to the quality of our lives, so if you have friends who love and care about you, you are truly blessed.

Saturday — *September 26*

OUR friend Isobel was telling me about a collection of letters written by women to their younger selves, full of advice and wisdom that they wished they could have possessed at the time.

I'm sure many of us look back on our earlier years and wish that we had sometimes acted with a little more insight. But I'm not sure that wisdom is always just one-way traffic from Age to Youth.

Youth can often teach Age a thing or two, for example, qualities like idealism. Perhaps the best state of mind to adopt is if we remember that we can all learn from each other, whatever our age!

Sunday — *September 27*

WE may wonder why a loving God allows suffering. Well, let me relate this little story.

Puzzled by a reference to God as a "purifier of silver" a group of students visited a silversmith and asked to watch the process. He explained that the raw silver must be held in the hottest part of the flame to weaken it and burn away the impurities. Afterwards the metal would be fashioned into something beautiful, but if he didn't sit near the flame and pay close attention it might easily overheat and be wasted.

One of the group asked, "How do you recognise the moment of purification?"

"Oh, that's easy," the silversmith said. "It's when I can see my image reflected in it."

"He shall sit as a refiner and purifier of silver and He shall purify the sons of Levi and purge them as gold and silver, that they may offer unto the Lord an offering in righteousness."

(Malachi 3:3)

Monday — *September 28*

WHEN things don't go the way we want them to, we can react in one of two ways. We can sit down and cry — or we can work to make things better.

Jesse Jackson put it like this: "Both sweat and tears are salty, but they render a different result. Tears will get you sympathy; sweat will get you change."

The choice is yours.

Tuesday — *September 29*

DAVE and Della are the sort of people who have a real knack with young people and, after having their own family, have happily fostered many more children over the years.

Dave, however, would be the first to admit that there is a limit to his other talents. An attempt to get to grips with watercolour painting wasn't entirely successful, a fact confirmed when one of the youngest boys had to ask what Dave's picture of a boat was actually meant to be.

Della couldn't help but smile, yet still managed to lighten his gloom when she came up with a quotation from Vincent van Gogh, who said, "I tell you, the more I think, the more I feel that there is nothing more truly artistic than to love people."

"In which case," Della said to her husband, "I vote you a real old master."

Wednesday — *September 30*

WE know that we cannot live by bread alone. It is right that we should also remember all those who have no bread at all.

October

Thursday — **October 1**

IT seemed a bit strange at first. The instructions on Jim's new camcorder suggested letting the battery run down completely once in a while before recharging it. Apparently this would increase the battery's endurance.

Then I thought of people I know who have lived easy lives and who find the slightest upheaval quite traumatic. But I also know folk who have faced severe trials. At the time their hardships seemed cruel and pointless, draining those involved of every last reserve, but afterwards I found I had friends with a greater endurance of suffering and a greater capacity for love.

Who would have thought you'd find an old-fashioned parable hidden in such state-of-the-art technology?

Friday — **October 2**

SIMON was having a stressful day until he came across this wonderful quote from Loretta LaRoche that lifted his spirits and helped put everything into perspective:

"Love often, laugh a lot, make gratitude your daily companion, take good care of yourself, catch people doing something right, and find something to bless in the mess."

Saturday — **October 3**

AN Australian friend tells me the highest compliment an Aborigine can pay someone who has passed on is to say, "They walked gently on the earth." By this they mean the person did no damage to the world and treated it with respect.

It's an example worth emulating, not only with the physical world. In our time we will pass through the lives and hearts of many people. How better to do that than to "walk gently"?

Sunday — **October 4**

HERE is a Victorian child's prayer to share with you today:

Matthew, Mark, Luke, and John,
Bless the bed that I lie on.
Four corners to my bed,
Four Angels there be spread:
One at my head, one at my feet,
And two to guard me while I sleep.
God within and God without,
And Jesus Christ all round about;
If any danger come to me,
Sweet Jesus Christ deliver me.
Before I lay me down to sleep,
I give my soul to Christ to keep;
And if I die before I wake
I pray that Christ my soul will take.

Monday — **October 5**

NATURE and books belong to the eyes that see them.   Ralph Waldo Emerson.

THE FRIENDSHIP BOOK

Tuesday — **October 6**

PEOPLE seem to worry more than ever nowadays and sadly, it is nearly always unnecessary. This humorous verse says it all:

The worried cow would have lived till now
If she had saved her breath;
But she feared her hay wouldn't last all day,
And she mooed herself to death.

Mark Twain put it this way: "'Don't you worry and don't you hurry,' I know that phrase by heart, and if all the other music perish out of the world it would still sing to me."

Wednesday — **October 7**

MELLOW DAYS

AUTUMN in her russet robes
Comes dancing down the lane,
Touching every leaf and tree
She sets the woods aflame.
A magic mass of colour
Transforms the woodland scene,
To crimson, flame and yellow
Where everything was green.

Loveliest of seasons
Of mists and mellow days,
Where fruited boughs are laden
And fields of corn and maize,
Are ready for the gleaners
For harvest time is here,
And nature yields her blessing
Upon the dying year.
                    Kathleen Gillum.

Thursday — **October 8**

ONE night Frederick Charrington, of the famous brewery family, saw a woman pleading with her husband not to go into a public house. He went in, knocking down his young daughter as he went. Above the door Charrington read his own name.

From that night he decided that he would have nothing to do with the brewing trade. He moved into cheap lodgings in London's East End and spent his days and nights campaigning against the evils afflicting poor families.

In Mile End Road, in 1886, he opened a huge prayer hall and preached to the five thousand people who flocked to the meeting.

He fought hard against the exploitation of women and by the time he died the East End was a better, healthier and happier place thanks to his work.

Friday — **October 9**

PROGRESS . . . it has become rather a double-edged word, hasn't it? We have become suspicious of it because so often we expect it to mean change for the worse.

But let us remember that progress often brings change for the better. Just think of the improvements in medicine, in housing and many other fields.

Whatever we do, we can't stop it. Progress will continue no matter what we say or do.

So let's encourage those who are working to improve things. Everyone can help, even in a small way, to make the world a better place.

THE FRIENDSHIP BOOK

Saturday — **October 10**

"THERE is nothing on this earth to be prized more than true friendship." St Thomas Aquinas.

Sunday — **October 11**

BEING awarded an Oscar has to be the high point of any actor's career. Dame Helen Mirren was no less delighted than any other winner when she accepted her statuette, but afterwards she had this advice for reporters:

"It's incredibly exciting, but it's fleeting and one has to recognise that. You have to enjoy the moment and then let it go."

Awards are all very well, but they are transient. For a prize that will last forever we should look elsewhere.

Do not store up for yourselves treasures on earth, where moth and rust destroy and where thieves break in and steal, but store up for yourselves treasures in Heaven, where moth and rust do not destroy and where thieves do not break in and steal. For where your treasure is, there your heart will be also. (Matthew 6: 19-21)

Monday — **October 12**

THE writer George Elliot said: "It will never rain roses, if you want more roses, you must plant more trees." This is wise advice as it simply means don't just sit there — get up and do something to make your dream come true.

Take whatever action you can to achieve your goal. Determination, clear focus and plenty of elbow grease are necessary tools.

So go and plant your rose bush!

Tuesday — **October 13**

*T*HIS is the day to start anew
And make those hidden dreams come true,
To find a smoother path to tread
And see the rainbow up ahead.
This is the day to lend a hand
Let someone know you understand,
A time to give, a time to share,
And show the troubled world you care.
A day to seek once more and find
A ray of hope and peace of mind,
To count your blessings, one by one,
Enjoying rain and wind and sun.
Step out with joy along your way,
This is the time, this is the day!

Iris Hesselden.

Wednesday — **October 14**

YOU may have heard of the Italian Chapel in Orkney. During the Second World War Italian prisoners of war lovingly converted two corrugated iron Nissen huts into a beautiful place of worship that still stands even though the rest of the camp is long gone.

What I didn't know was that the statue of St George slaying the dragon outside the chapel was meant to signify the prisoners' triumph over defeat and loneliness. This statue is made from concrete which needed some kind of internal metal framework. So what did these ingenious craftsmen use? Barbed wire. The same barbed wire that ringed their camp!

When the human spirit is in search of freedom and spiritual uplift can anything hold it prisoner?

THE FRIENDSHIP BOOK

Thursday — **October 15**

THE writer P. G. Wodehouse was only two when his mother brought him back to England from Hong Kong where his father was a civil servant. She rented a house in Bath, hired someone to look after him and did not see him again for several years.

When he was old enough his parents had him enrolled at a boarding school. Holidays were spent with relatives or friends. There was never a single place he could call home.

The wonder is that he never showed any bitterness but, instead, went on to write some of the funniest books in the English language, creating characters such as Jeeves and Bertie Wooster who are still entertaining us today.

Friday — **October 16**

RICHARD hung a poster with these thought-provoking statements in his office. He says they compel him to approach each day's events, large and small, with vision:

*I asked for strength and I was given difficulties
to make me strong.
I asked for wisdom and was given problems
to solve.
I asked for prosperity and was given energy
to work.
I asked for courage and was given obstacles
to overcome.
I asked for love and was given people to help.
I asked for favours and was given opportunities.
I received nothing I wanted, but everything
I needed.*

Saturday — *October 17*

WHAT is your favourite time of day? When someone asked me that I found it very difficult to answer.

Sunrise is filled with hope, midday a sort of lull between the activity of the morning and the afternoon. Evening gives us a chance to wind down and reflect on the past hours, and then comes night offering us rest and the balm of sleep.

The truth is that every day brings us fresh opportunities, pleasures old and new, and the secret is, I believe, never to be so busy that we do not see and appreciate the beauties and wonders of this amazing world around us.

Sunday — *October 18*

SUNDAY . . . "Day of the Lord, as all our days should be!" Henry Wadsworth Longfellow.

Monday — *October 19*

CHATTING with a farmer friend Donald, I commented on how beautiful everything looked with a fresh sprinkling of frost. "It's more than just nice," he informed me. "It's essential."

He went on to explain how a hard frost breaks down the heavy clumps of ploughed earth making the sowing of crops much easier and it also takes care of many of the harmful bugs that hibernate all Winter, ones which can damage new crops.

Frost is just one of the many things I'd taken for granted, but to those in the know it seems there's a good reason for every little thing. Almost as if it was planned, in fact.

Tuesday — **October 20**

I READ about a man who conquered Everest — and in doing so added his discarded oxygen cylinders to the refuse littering the mountain's slopes.

Not content with this sight, he went back and started gathering up some of the debris. He melted down the aluminium cylinders and fashioned them into works of art which he then sold for Nepalese charities.

Now, that's what I call a fine example of the philosophy for life which advises, "Give more than you take, fix more than you break."

Wednesday — **October 21**

ATTENDING a theatre performance one evening, our old friend Mary found her attention drawn to the musicians sitting under the stage. They were in darkness, with tiny lights illuminating their sheet music. They couldn't see what was going on above them, but by following the conductor's lead they played an integral part in the performance.

"You know, Francis," Mary told me later. "We have our own 'sheet music', or instructions on how to play, in the form of the Bible. We often don't know what's going on outside our little circle but we do have Someone who sees both above and below to guide us.

"There's a lot we can't see and we might often feel left in the dark, but by watching the conductor we can each of us add our own beautiful music to the bigger show."

Now, that's surely something well worth thinking about today.

Thursday — **October 22**

DAVE came across this thought-provoking sentence in a magazine: *A path with no obstacles probably doesn't lead anywhere.*

A fine piece of advice to keep in mind.

Friday — **October 23**

TIME TO SAIL

LAP, lap, the wavelets slap
  Against the painted hulls,
The creek is full of bobbing boats,
  And cries of wheeling gulls.
The air is clear, the wind is fresh,
  The tide runs swift and free,
As if to bid the tethered craft
  Set sail and come with me!
For who, on such a day as this
  Would choose to stay safe moored,
When such a wide and wondrous world
  Just waits to be explored?

Margaret Ingall.

Saturday — **October 24**

AT seventy years of age Kris Kristofferson had been a singer/songwriter for almost half a century. Talking about the good times and the bad, he described what had sustained him.

"The faith of my father got me this far," he said. "The smiles of my children will take me the rest of the way."

In little words, big truths can be hiding from all of us. I've yet to hear a better description of how we all are, in the end, one large, ongoing, eternal family.

Sunday — **October 25**

"SHINE, Jesus Shine". If you're familiar with that hymn, then I expect you find, like me, that a robust rendition can bring light to the gloomiest day!

You may also know that it's just one of many pieces of music written by Graham Kendrick, a Baptist pastor's son who trained as a teacher until he decided to trust instead in his natural talent and make a career as a professional musician.

"Shine, Jesus Shine" is possibly his best-loved hymn, although it didn't have a promising beginning. Its first few airings passed without it making any kind of impact and it wasn't until its composer — himself unsure of its merits — thought of adding a chorus that it really took off.

Nowadays, like many of his works, it is sung the world over, bringing pleasure to millions, and reminding us of the words of our Lord:

I have come into the world as a light, so that no-one who believes in me should stay in darkness.
(John 12:46)

Monday — **October 26**

WRITER and artist Denton Welch was still an art student when, one day in 1935, he was knocked off his bicycle by a careless driver. For the rest of his life he was a semi-invalid, often in pain and discomfort.

For a time he avoided company, seeking to be left alone, until he realised his mistake. To a friend he wrote this: "If one does no good, gives no happiness, goes out to no-one, what is the point of living at all?"

Tuesday — *October 27*

FRIENDS just back from a holiday in Canada were enthusing about the mighty Niagara Falls. But one was more taken with something far less magnificent.

Before the Welland River joins the Niagara it's quite safe for boating, but afterwards . . . That's where Joanne had noticed the signs. Fixed to a bridge over the river was the warning, *Do You Have An Anchor? Do You Know How To Use It?*

Turbulent spiritual currents might be close to even the quietest life. That's why it's priceless to have faith as a strong anchor — and be practised in using it!

Wednesday — *October 28*

MOIRA and Yvonne have been friends for a long time. They first met as schoolgirls and their rapport has endured over many years, weathering adolescent rivalry, the commitment of marriage and children and even a disagreement or two.

Moira celebrated her seventieth birthday, and showed me a card from Yvonne, in which were written some words from writer Dorothy Rowe:

Friendships are distinguished by trust, loyalty, affection and a similar outlook on life, but there is more than that. There is the quality of timelessness. This is how things are. The sun rises, the wind blows, and we are friends.

That kind of relationship is a gift for life!

Thursday — *October 29*

BEGIN to weave and God will give you the thread. German Proverb.

Friday — *October 30*

HERE'S a wise set of instructions that arrived by e-mail. Think about them today.

Be yourself — Truthfully
Accept yourself — Gracefully
Value yourself — Joyfully
Forgive yourself — Completely
Treat yourself — Generously
Balance yourself — Harmoniously
Bless yourself — Abundantly
Trust yourself — Confidently
Love yourself — Wholeheartedly
Empower yourself — Prayerfully
Give yourself — Enthusiastically
Express yourself — Radiantly.

Saturday — *October 31*

CAN you picture the magnificence of a giant redwood tree? So tall, so strong, so independent?

You would imagine the roots of such a tree would run deep below the ground and each tree would stand alone, but, no. The roots stay near the surface to gather maximum rainfall and intertwine with the roots of other redwoods. Much of the strength needed to keep them upright in windy weather comes from the shared, hidden strength of their neighbours.

We, too, should remember that we are each interconnected as individuals by a system of roots and, as part of a family, a work team, a neighbourhood or a community, we can stand tall and come through the stormy weather together.

November

*G*OD, I pray you'll grant to me
    A fair share of humility,
Let me live my life to be
    With diffidence and modesty.

Be gracious Lord and teach to me
    The meaning of servility,
Open my eyes and let me see
    The world does not revolve round me.

Let me serve You in all I do
    My faith and love of You renew
Let me recall what is so true
    That I am nothing, without You.

                    Colin Hammacott.

I'M sure you know the kind of people I have in mind today. No matter how dark the clouds they always manage to find a little sunshine.

Recalling her early life as a young black girl in America's segregated south, Maya Angelou describes good cheer in the face of adversity this way:

"The caged bird doesn't sing because it has an answer: it sings because it has a song."

Do you have a song to sing?

THE FRIENDSHIP BOOK

Tuesday — **November 3**

A WELL-KNOWN sports magazine ran this quote on success: *What counts most in creating a successful team is not how compatible the players are, but how they deal with incompatibility.*

Whether your team is a family, an office or a neighbourhood it's your understanding and caring for the shortcomings of others (and theirs for you) that will make yours a truly winning combination!

Wednesday — **November 4**

VAL met young Andrew and his mother on their way home from nursery.

"Did you have a nice time today, Andrew?" she asked.

"Yes, it was fantastic!" he enthused.

"What did you do?" she enquired, thinking that something exciting must have happened — an outing, perhaps, or a prize for work well done.

After some thought, he replied, "Oh, nothing special, it was just all fantastic."

As Val went on her way, she mulled over his reaction and what makes a "fantastic" day. In these times of endless aspiration and material expectations we are often encouraged to believe we need big rewards and special treats to be happy. Many people seem to want more and more.

However, that's not the way to true and lasting happiness. If we can foster the attitude displayed by Andrew, perhaps we can begin to appreciate everyday pleasures and successes more, and see every day as "fantastic".

THE FRIENDSHIP BOOK

Thursday — **November 5**

SOME folk seem to spend their lives living in the past, but often it's a past that never really was, concentrating only on the good parts they choose to recall. Other people live their lives for the future yet no matter how hard they try, the future rarely turns out the way they had hoped.

Well, if you can't rely on the past or the future and the present is ever fleeting, what else can you do?

Charlotte Brontë may just have had the right idea when she said, "I try to avoid looking forward or backward, and try to keep looking upward."

Friday — **November 6**

THE sweetest pleasures of this world
Are those we all can share —
The joyful sound of laughter,
Or the smell of rain-washed air.
We all can taste an apple
Or can feel the sun's warm rays,
Or look to see the dancing skies
On blue and windy days.
And knowing that these simple joys
Are understood by all
Increases every happiness,
Each pleasure large or small.

Margaret Ingall.

Saturday — **November 7**

OUR old friend Mary likes this thought-provoking saying — and so do I!
We can't all be stars, but we can all twinkle.

STANDING STONES

Sunday — **November 8**

NOVEMBER can be a dark and dispiriting month, said Susan's clergyman to his congregation one Sunday, because of the onset of Winter, an often dull time before the build-up to Christmas.

Then he spoke of All Saints' Day and how it is a time to remember those who have passed on. "I think of the many families down the centuries who have worshipped here," he said.

"And I like to think that we, who are here now feel touched in some way by the presence of all those from the long-distant past."

Susan recalled the words of St Paul, in Corinthians II, 5:1 "For we know that if our earthly house of this tabernacle were dissolved, we have a building of God, an house not made with hands, eternal in the heavens."

Monday — **November 9**

GAIL'S mother always gives her this advice when she complains that things aren't going exactly as planned: "A contented person is one who enjoys the scenery along the detours!"

Tuesday — **November 10**

I SMILED broadly when I read this description of a victorious Roman general entering a city. His captives led the procession, then came scores of carts bearing the treasure he had taken.

One servant guided the horses, while the other whispered, "Remember, you're only human."

Next time we're tempted to become too big for our boots, let's recall these wise words.

Wednesday — **November 11**

IN the Staffordshire countryside, near Lichfield, lies the National Memorial Arboretum, a tranquil spot dotted with memorials standing beneath thousands of trees. They remember the countless individuals who gave their lives in past wars.

There are stones or groves of trees in memory of all the different services and, in addition, others such as those who died in the troubled years in Northern Ireland, war widows and other civilian groups.

Visitors can sit quietly in the gardens or in the chapel where services are held. At a solemn moment every day the Reveille and Last Post are sounded. This is a place where we can truly say the brave are never forgotten.

Thursday — **November 12**

"I WAS going to look up the meaning of the word 'procrastination'," Lewis said, "but then I decided I'd put it off for a while."

It's a good joke but, to be a little more serious, procrastination can be an attitude which is all too easy to fall into. We tell ourselves that another day will do, and dream of how perfect life will be when we've achieved our goals — but sadly, never quite get round to taking the steps that will actually lead us there.

Leo Buscaglia, a teacher and writer, put it succinctly: "Life lived for tomorrow will always be just a day away from being realised," he said.

So let's try to start fully living life now. No, I don't mean after we've done the crossword, ambled round the garden, and made a second cup of tea . . .

Friday — **November 13**

I HAPPENED upon these words by Nathaniel Cotton which I'd like to share with you. He had this to say about prayer:

"This is that incense of the heart, whose fragrance smells to Heaven."

He was an 18th-century physician and poet.

Saturday — **November 14**

KAREEN Kohn has no address. He is a nomad, a man who travels all over the world. As founder of Nomads United he takes small groups of people on horseback through remote areas in Latin America and Asia. These trips will last about three months and each of the participants is asked to purchase his or her own horse and materials.

Along the way the nomads pitch their tents, but sometimes they find a place to stay in a village in the mountains. The group performs for the villagers — dancing, making music or juggling — in exchange for a place to sleep and food for the horses. Nomads United exchanges ideas with the locals on ecological awareness, respect and care for animals and nature.

Kareen once said, "We attempt to change people's perspective on their relationship with earth and its creatures. You can't see the stars in the city.

"I dream that in two hundred years the cities will be empty. And that, as nomads, we will pass by and think, how on earth could people have lived caged like this while there is so much beauty everywhere?"

Sunday — **November 15**

LLOYD Douglas, author of "The Robe", once shared lodgings with a wheelchair-bound music professor. One day he asked the professor, "What's the good news this morning?"

The professor tapped a tuning fork on his wheelchair and replied, "That's Middle C. It was Middle C yesterday and it will still be Middle C a thousand years from now."

The world is changing faster than ever before. Fashions change, technology changes, even the weather seems to be changing. What we need is a "Middle C", something, or someone, that always was and always will be there, no matter what else changes.

David, the great Psalmist, points us in the direction of just such certainty: "From everlasting to everlasting, You are God."

Monday — **November 16**

HERE'S a message that arrived in our friend Linda's e-mail box one morning and made her workload seem lighter and the day brighter:

Life is short, break the rules: forgive quickly, kiss slowly, love truly, laugh uncontrollably and never regret anything that made you smile!

Tuesday — **November 17**

OUR friend Adrian said that whenever life becomes more than just a little challenging, he remembers this wise saying:

A diamond is a chunk of coal that was made good under pressure.

SUNSET SCENE

THE FRIENDSHIP BOOK

Wednesday — **November 18**

"LITTLE things please little minds." So often that phrase is used rather scathingly, yet I sometimes wonder why. Nobel Prize-winning poet Pablo Neruda certainly didn't think that small things were beneath his notice.

No-one could accuse this Chilean writer of leading a simple life, for his involvement in politics and human rights frequently led him into conflict and complications. Yet still his poems urge us to notice even the most humdrum items — lemons, bees, coal sacks and stamp albums all featured in his writing.

The act of creating poetry, he felt, was to enter a partnership of "solitude and solidarity, emotion and action, the nearness to oneself, the nearness to mankind . . ."

Pablo Neruda died in 1973, and by using his talent to celebrate the wonder of the everyday items around us, he left us all a valuable legacy. Nothing in the world is so ordinary that we should take it for granted.

Thursday — **November 19**

I CAME across this rhyme and it reminded me that friendship is one of life's special joys:
Man strives for glory, honour, fame,
So that all the world may know his name,
Amasses wealth by brain and hand,
Becomes a power in the land.
But when he nears the end of life
And looks back over the years of strife
He finds that happiness depends
On none of these, but love of friends.

Friday — **November 20**

RICHARD CARLSON tells us about simple ways to keep little things from overtaking your life. Here are some of the suggestions he offers to help put things into perspective and make life calmer.

Develop compassion; make peace with imperfection; let others have the glory; breathe before you speak; nurture a plant; be happy where you are; choose being kind over being right; schedule time for your inner work.

Saturday — **November 21**

LAUGHTER is the sun that drives Winter from your face.

Sunday — **November 22**

WITH so many people in need, "How best to help?" is a question that often seems difficult.

Thomas was determined he would be a medical missionary to China, but while studying he became involved with the plight of homeless children. He was torn between his original ambition and his new vocation until a particular extract from the Bible seemed to offer a solution.

Two days later he received an anonymous and substantial donation for his work with children, provided he stayed to administrate it.

"I did not choose this path," Thomas Barnardo, founder of Dr Barnardo's Homes said, "My Father called me."

And the extract from the Bible? It was Psalm 33, verse 8: "I will instruct thee in the way thou shalt go, I will guide thee with mine eyes."

Monday — **November 23**

*Y*OU said you'd burned your bridges,
   Now there's no turning back,
Your future so uncertain
   Your life is not on track.
You're not quite sure which way to go,
   The signpost out of view,
The road is steep and rocky
   The sky no longer blue.
But now it's time to start again,
   For this is not the end,
Remember all those happy times
   And build a bridge, my friend.

                          Iris Hesselden.

Tuesday — **November 24**

I LIKE this entry found in Great-Aunt Louisa's diary: "24th November. — After a week of gentle sun and mild air, we had our first real taste of Winter today, sharp showers of sleety rain driven by a blustery wind. Yet late in the afternoon I looked up from my easel to see a rainbow in the sky, surely beautiful enough to hide a pot of gold at the end. It reminded me of something I'd once read:

After a day of cloud and wind and rain,
Sometimes the setting sun breaks out again
And, touching all the darksome woods with light,
Smiles on the fields, until they laugh and sing,
Then like a ruby from horizon's ring,
Drops down into the night.

These lines by Longfellow remind us of Nature's wonders, which lift the heart and bring us joy."

Wednesday — **November 25**

LAURA always had the television on at home, or the radio playing loudly in her car. She scarcely even noticed what was on as she'd become so accustomed to all the background noise. But then, a friend's comment made her re-evaluate and change her habit.

"I need to be able to hear the sound of my heartbeat in the silence," she said. "That's the best way for me to be focused and calm."

Minnie Aumonier once said, "There is always music amongst the trees in the garden, but our hearts must be very quiet to hear it."

Enjoy the silence.

Thursday — **November 26**

THANKSGIVING DAY is a time when Americans remember the founders of their nation. These ill-prepared settlers almost starved, but native Americans showed them how to plant crops and fed the new arrivals until a harvest could be gathered. In return they were invited to a three-day feast of thanksgiving.

The tradition starts there, but the story does not end there. Many more settlers arrived. Supplies were scarce, crops failed and many died.

Two hard years later another celebration took place. Founding Father William Bradford wrote in his diary: "A solemn day was set apart wherein we returned glory, honour and praise, with all thankfulness, to our God who dwelt so graciously with us."

From such optimism in the midst of real hardship, the United States was born.

Friday — **November 27**

FORGIVENESS has been described "like the fragrance of a rose that rises to bless the foot that crushes".

We all know we should forgive our enemies, yet we can find this difficult and carry on harbouring grudges. Bitter thoughts and feelings can so easily entrap us and with the passing of time they can be deeply embedded. The longer we leave it the harder it becomes to let go.

In the wise words of Madame de Stael, nineteenth-century writer and the first woman to be officially recognised as a political philosopher: "To understand is to pardon."

How good it is to begin to put grudges behind us, for who would want to live in the shadows when we can choose to step out and live in the sunshine?

Saturday — **November 28**

OUR friend Gladys hadn't heard of Buy Nothing Day until, one late Saturday in November, she met some young acquaintances. They were handing out leaflets and told her that the idea was for this one day, people should resist shopping and think instead of those throughout the world who have nothing.

Buy Nothing Day was started in 1993 and is now recognised in over 50 countries. Instead of spending money, those who have it try to spend time — with family or friends, or doing something that costs nothing such as walking, gardening or reading.

That can't be bad, can it?

THE FRIENDSHIP BOOK

Sunday — *November 29*

IN Sunday schools children sing "All Things Bright And Beautiful" with as much enthusiasm as those for whom it was written more than one hundred and fifty years ago. "There Is A Green Hill Far Away" and "Jesus Calls Us O'er The Tumult" are still popular, and what carol concert would seem complete without "Once In Royal David's City"?

These and many more were written by a painfully shy and short-sighted Irish girl, Cecil Frances Alexander, born in 1823. She married Rev. William Alexander who became Primate of all Ireland.

Her "Hymns For Little Children" ran to one hundred editions, all profit going to a Londonderry school for deaf mutes. She was rightly described as "a pearl among women".

Monday — *November 30*

I'VE heard it said that Indian corn tends to do poorly in the intense noonday heat, growing better in the balmy nights. Coral reefs which shelter so many islands are more alive and vibrant on the side battered by ocean currents. And the evening primrose only shows its true beauty as shadows lengthen.

Often, I think, the things we might consider trials or hindrances have their purpose. We just don't always see life that way, at least at first. Henry Jackson Van Dyke wrote:

If all of life were sunshine
Our face would long to gain
And feel once more upon it
The cooling splash of rain.

December

*E*ACH life is like a jigsaw
  With pieces large and small,
Some fragments show a pattern,
  But others not at all.
Yet still we try to fit them,
  To make a picture grow,
We puzzle and we ponder,
  What meaning they might show.
Yet some day, if we're patient,
  And truth remains our goal,
I'm sure we'll see these pieces
  Have made a perfect whole.

Margaret Ingall.

HERE are some thoughts to share with you on a Winter's day:

"The ageing process has you firmly in its grasp if you never get the urge to throw a snowball."

Douglas Larson.

With the infant harvest, breathing soft below
Its eider coverlet of snow,
Nor is in field or garden anything
But, duly look'd into, contains serene
The substance of things hoped for in the Spring.

Coventry Patmore.

Thursday — **December 3**

" I LIKE to be independent." It was one of Enid's favourite phrases, and while it's a perfectly good sentiment, it can sometimes be a disadvantage, as she began to realise when she broke her hip and found herself struggling to come to terms with the fact that she had to rely on others.

"At first I felt awkward about needing so much help," she said. "But then slowly I discovered that it wasn't just a one-way process. Often my carers told me how fulfilling they found their role, while others said how rewarding it was to be able to repay the help I'd given them in the past. You know, if it hadn't been for my mishap, I wouldn't have realised just how rich in friends I am."

Sometimes it's not until we lose something of value that we realise we have gained an even greater gift.

Friday — **December 4**

L IFE is a journey. I think we can all agree on that. It's only when we start debating the purpose of that journey or the final destination that we may differ.

Life can at times seem frustrating, even pointless, which is why our friend Peter laughed with delight — and understanding — when he read the following exchange between two of author George McDonald's characters.

"I wonder why God made me," said one. "I certainly don't see any purpose in it!"

"Perhaps you don't see any purpose in it yet," replied his friend, "But then, He hasn't finished making you."

Saturday — **December 5**

I'M sure we'd all like to do our bit to improve the world. Many of us will no doubt look with awe at the men and women who walk away from everyday lives, even high-powered jobs, then spend years in self-sacrificing devotion to a worthwhile cause. However, with the best will in the world, that's not for everyone.

What can the rest of us do? Well, Howard Thurman had this advice:

"Don't ask what the world needs. Ask what makes you come alive — and go do it. Because what the world needs most is people who have come alive!"

Sunday — **December 6**

HERE'S something for us to think about today. What would happen if we treated our Bibles in the same way as we treat our mobile phones?

What if we wore the Bible on a belt, or carried it in our handbag or a pocket? What if we flipped through it several times a day? What if we used it to receive messages from the text? What if we treated it as if we couldn't live without it?

Unlike a mobile phone, we don't ever have to worry about the Bible losing its connection, or having to be recharged.

I hope this message prompts you to open your Bible today — and tomorrow, and the day after . . .

Monday — **December 7**

"SHUN idleness. It is a rust that attaches itself to the most brilliant metals."

Voltaire.

SNOW BRIGHT

Tuesday — **December 8**

THE Lady of the House came home smiling one afternoon.

"I've just been talking to Anna — you know how methodical she is. Well, she was telling me about labelling her home-made freezer meals, like 'Chicken Tikka Masala' or 'Beef Bourguignon.' However, whenever she asked her husband what he fancied to eat from her list he didn't really answer her.

"In desperation, Anna decided to stock up with his various replies. Nowadays her freezer is full of dinners with neat little tags that say, 'Whatever', 'I Don't Know', 'Something Good', or 'I Don't Mind'.

"So now, Francis, there's no more frustration for Anna because whatever her husband answers when she asks him what he'd like for dinner, it's there, ready and waiting. Isn't that innovative of her?

I had to agree!

Wednesday — **December 9**

I WAS amused to read about two friends who, as a joke, take it in turn every Christmas to exchange a china ornament so unattractive that neither would want to keep it.

I suspect quite a few of us have, on occasion, received the sort of gift which, however well meant, will never take pride of place on our mantelpiece.

It reminded me of some words credited to Cort Flint: "It is difficult to give away kindness. It keeps coming back to you."

Thursday — **December 10**

GWEN was trying to encourage her grand-daughter who was facing a daunting number of school exams. "I think I left her feeling more positive," she smiled. "Especially when I told her the rhyme that my own grandmother taught me years ago:

You feel your fears have grown so large
They darken all the sky?
Then feed your faith and you will see
How fear will starve and die!

That truth will never become old-fashioned.

Friday — **December 11**

HERE is a small bouquet of thoughts for December. This month sees Advent, a time of preparation for the birth of the Christchild at Bethlehem, a time when calendars are opened to mark the passing of the days and wreaths are made of evergreens.

December sees both the shortest day around 22nd and the beginning, after this, of the WInter solstice, the slow but sure return of longer, daylight hours.

December treasures include the stars which seem to sparkle their brightest on clear, frosty nights, and let's not forget the joy of the first Christmas rose — creamy-white and tinged with pink — in a corner of the garden.

And with goodwill towards others so much a part of the season, what better to keep in mind than these words by Albert Watson:

And every day throughout the year
Keep Christmas in your heart.

Saturday — **December 12**

HAVE you heard about Maisie DeVore, who donated enough money to her town to enable the residents to build a swimming pool?

How generous, you may think, but presumably she had plenty of money — perhaps she was an entrepreneur, an heiress, or even a lottery winner?

In fact, Maisie is a senior citizen, who just happens to have spent the past thirty years picking up abandoned aluminium cans and taking them to be recycled, until eventually she raised the six-figure sum needed to pay for the town's pool.

Next time you think your efforts are too small to improve anything, remember Maisie. With determination, anyone can jump in and make a splash in the world!

Sunday — **December 13**

" THE Sunday is the core of our civilisation, dedicated to thought and reverence."
Ralph Waldo Emerson.

Monday — **December 14**

WE are spoiled for choice with the range of greeting cards available these days. We have pop-up ones, musical ones and even online ones we can personalise. But, as with so many other things, the simplest is often the best.

I especially like this little verse from an old Christmas card. The unknown writer said:
It's an old, old wish
On a tiny little card —
It's simply Merry Christmas
But I wish it very hard!

Tuesday — **December 15**

*T*HE world is filled with magic,
  Waiting quietly, patiently
For an unsuspecting soul
To unleash its beauty.
Dare to risk;
Forgive often,
Speak gentle words,
Give to those who ask,
Leave the safe harbour.
Dare to believe;
Dream without restraint,
Love much,
Dress yourself in courage,
Be the poem you long to read
And the enchanted secrets,
Magical adventures
And happy endings
You thought existed only in fairytales
Will come true.
                    Rachel Wallace-Oberle.

Wednesday — **December 16**

WILLIAM Bernard Ullathorne started off his working life as a cabin boy at sea and ended up as a highly-respected churchman!

Quite how he made it from start to finish is a fascinating story and I'm sure that his sunny personality helped smooth the way. His outlook is summed up in these words which we can all take to heart:

"Nothing contributes more to cheerfulness than the habit of looking at the good side of things. The good side is, after all, God's side."

Thursday — **December 17**

A READER has sent me an Irish blessing for the season of Advent:

"May peace and plenty be the first to lift the latch to your door and happiness be guided to your home by the candle of Christmas."

I think it sums up all we could wish for each other.

Friday — **December 18**

" IT wouldn't be Christmas without this," said the radio presenter as he played Bing Crosby's classic version of the song "White Christmas".

There's no denying that Mr Crosby had one of the outstanding singing voices of the twentieth century. But no matter how well he sang the real magic of the song doesn't come out until he is joined by the strings of the orchestra and his backing singers.

And that's the secret of Christmas! It's something one person can't do justice to, something you don't get the full benefit of until you share it.

So if you know someone who might be spending Christmas on their own, why don't you join them or invite them along to your celebrations? Christmas isn't really about songs, or presents, or snow — it's about sharing.

Saturday — **December 19**

" EVERYBODY needs beauty as well as bread, places to play in and pray in, where nature may heal and give strength to body and soul."

John Muir.

THE FRIENDSHIP BOOK

Sunday — **December 20**

PHILLIPS Brooks admitted to being a failure as a teacher yet he was to become the Bishop of Massachusetts. He was born in Boston in 1835, educated at Harvard and at the Episcopal Theological Seminary in Virginia.

You haven't heard of him? Maybe not, but you're sure to have sung the much-loved lines he wrote after visiting the birthplace of Jesus. They begin:

O little town of Bethlehem
How still we see thee lie;
Above thy deep and dreamless sleep
The silent stars go by.

Monday — **December 21**

ALWAYS face the sunshine and the shadows will fall behind.

Tuesday — **December 22**

ARE you having a challenging day because of some upset in your relations with a friend or colleague?

Or, on the other side of the coin, has someone shown you the best side of their character and left you feeling grateful for a special good turn?

I came across these words one day and I think they sum up both contrasting events:

"When someone hurts us we should write it down in sand, where winds of forgiveness can erase it away. But, when someone does something good for us, we must engrave it in stone where no wind can ever erase it."

Wednesday — **December 23**

HAVE you heard of the Society of Mary and Martha? For some years it has been providing respite for those worn down by the commitments of caring for others.

This Society helps clergymen and women — in fact, anyone — turn a personal breakdown into a personal breakthrough. How do they achieve this? By providing a place to rest and get away from it all at their retreat centre in a converted farmhouse on the edge of Dartmoor.

They call it a twelve thousand-mile service, and the Sheldon Centre provides the perfect place to unwind. No-one is obliged to do anything! The spirit of the home at Bethany in which Jesus used to receive hospitality is upheld.

This haven provides a life-affirming opportunity for many in search of a fresh start.

Thursday — **December 24**

HOW often have you heard it said — "I wish every day could be like Christmas." Well, who says it can't?

Sports commentator Joe Garagiola was a big fan of legendary baseball player and coach "Yogi" Berra. Talking of his enthusiasm and the sheer delight he took from life, Garagiola described Berra like this: "One of those Christmas Eve guys. There are people like that . . . every day in their lives is like Christmas Eve!"

So, it seems every day can be like Christmas after all. If you have room enough in your heart you can carry it with you from one festive season to the next.

Friday — **December 25**

VILLAGE hall bedecked with holly
Waits for Santa, round and jolly,
Hills are silent, still and cold,
Sheep all gathered in the fold.

Smiling children, rosy faces
Hidden gifts in secret places,
Looking for a star so bright
Waiting now for Christmas night.

Lamps are shining everywhere,
Warmth and love for all to share,
Welcome in the village street,
Friends returning, friends to greet.

Homeward footsteps through the snow —
Country Christmas long ago.

Iris Hesselden.

Saturday — **December 26**

BARBARA loves books. Her most precious possession is an old and well-thumbed edition of that perennial tale of joy and hopefulness "Anne Of Green Gables" by Lucy M. Montgomery.

"Long ago," Barbara explained, "I had a schoolfriend who shared my affection for 'Anne Of Green Gables', and we would take it in turn to borrow it from the library.

"Eventually her family left the area, but before she went she saved up to buy me my own copy for my birthday and inside wrote a quotation from it: *Good friends are always together in spirit.*

"This book may have been written with children in mind, but it contains wisdom for all ages."

CHRISTMAS TREE

Sunday — *December 27*

THE Christmas truce during the First World War, when the British and German soldiers met for a game of football between the trenches is a well-known true story. I read about a similar happening in the Franco-Prussian war during the early 1870s.

In the still of that special evening the French troops sang, "Oh, Holy Night!" and from across the No Man's Land the Prussian troops responded with, "From Heaven Above To Earth I Come".

Whatever our circumstances the Holy Spirit is with us always.

Monday — *December 28*

WHY must we suffer? Well, I like the example given by M. R. DeHaan.

"A five dollar bar of steel when made into horseshoes is worth ten dollars. If the same bar is made into needles it's worth three hundred and fifty dollars. But if it's made into delicate springs for expensive watches its value rises to more than half a million dollars.

"The same bar of steel becomes more valuable by being cut up, passed through one furnace after another, hammered, manipulated, beaten, pounded and polished until it is ready for those delicate tasks."

I know the people I would best trust with "delicate tasks" have all been through life's mill.

Tuesday — *December 29*

IF we are facing in the right direction, all we have to do is keep on walking.

Buddha.

THE FRIENDSHIP BOOK

Wednesday — **December 30**

A S soon as the letter offering Jenny a new job arrived, doubts took over.

"I started to wonder if I really could do it," she confessed. "And then I came across this poem:

You want to see the vista
But you dare not climb the tower?
You long to pick the apple
But you won't in case it's sour?
Be brave, for trusting in yourself
Will always give you power:
The folk who reach the rainbow
Are the ones who brave the shower.

Jenny accepted the job — and loved it!

Thursday — **December 31**

A FELLOW statesman once asked Nelson Mandela how he'd managed not to be angry after spending decades in captivity.

He confessed that walking from his cell he had almost been consumed by anger, but he knew if he took the anger with him beyond the gates of his prison, those who had treated him badly would still have a hold on him.

"I wanted to be free," he said, "so I let it go. It was an astonishing moment in my life. It changed me."

Each New Year we anticipate the future, but ask yourself as the old year slips away, is there anything — a grudge, a row, a misunderstanding, that you can let go?

Then step into the year ahead as Mr Mandela stepped out into the sunshine. Free.

Photograph Locations and Photographers

DOUBLE TAKE — *River Avon, Chippenham.*
IN SAFE HANDS — *Mosaic, Patmos.*
NATURE'S POWER — *Goit Stock Waterfall, Bingley, West Yorkshire.*
DISCOVERY — *Dundee.*
CELTIC CONNECTIONS — *Whitby.*
FLORAL FRAME — *Edzell, Angus.*
BOATS OF MANY COLOURS — *Burano, Venice.*
BEYOND THE HORIZON — *Isle Of Coll.*
WALK ON — *Ullswater, Cumbria.*
RIVERSIDE RAMBLE — *Lower Slaughter, Cotswolds.*
POPPY DAY — *Crail, Fife.*
TRANQUIL WATERS — *Tal-y-Llyn, Gwynedd.*
AUTUMN'S RICHES — *Loch Rannoch, Perthshire.*
FAITH'S FOUNDATIONS — *Yosemite National Park, USA.*
STANDING STONES — *Kilchurn Castle, Loch Awe.*
SUNSET SCENE — *Barcelona.*
CHRISTMAS TREE — *Edinburgh.*

ACKNOWLEDGMENTS: **David Askham;** Boats Of Many Colours. **Matt Bain;** Strawberry Ice. **Ian Bayne;** Beyond The Horizon. **James D. Cameron;** Standing Stones. **Chris Cole**; Double Take. **Paul Felix;** Taking Shape, Tranquil Waters, Fine Tuning. **Colin Garthwaite;** Nature's Power, Top Marks. **V. K. Guy;** Walk On. **Margaret Ingall;** Snow Bright. **Martin Henderson Moar;** Home Sweet Home. **Duncan I. McEwan;** Autumn's Riches. **David Oakes;** Holding On. **Polly Pullar;** Faithful Companions. **Willie Shand;** Discovery. **Sheila Taylor;** Floral Frame, Bird's Eye-View, Riverside Ramble, Poppy Day, Faith's Foundations, Christmas Tree. **South West Images;** A Promise Of Spring, Blue Skye. **Travelscape Images;** In Safe Hands, Celtic Connections, House Proud, Sunset Scene. **Jack Watson;** Flight Of Fancy.

Printed and Published by D. C. Thomson & Co., Ltd.,
185 Fleet Street, London EC4A 2HS.
© D. C. Thomson & Co., Ltd., 2008